The Queen Who Ruled the Waves
and Other Amazing Tales of Royalty from Indian History

Indira Ananthakrishnan has been writing and telling stories for many years. She has written several award-winning short stories, historical tales, biographical sketches, plays and picture books. Her most recent book for Hachette India is *The Phoenix in the Sky: Tales of Wonder and Wisdom from World Religions* (2020). She has a special interest in interpreting the scriptures and happenings in history, and making them creatively appealing for young readers.

The Queen Who Ruled the Waves

and Other Amazing Tales of Royalty from Indian History

INDIRA ANANTHAKRISHNAN

illustrated by Priyanka Pachpande

hachette
INDIA

First published in 2022 by Hachette India
(Registered name: Hachette Book Publishing India Pvt. Ltd)
An Hachette UK company
www.hachetteindia.com

SRD

ISBN 978-93-91028-36-7

Hachette Book Publishing India Pvt. Ltd
4th & 5th Floors, Corporate Centre
Plot No. 94, Sector 44, Gurugram – 122003, India

Typeset by Manmohan Kumar, Delhi

Printed and bound in India
by Manipal Technologies Limited, Manipal

MIX
Paper from responsible sources
FSC™ C043100

CONTENTS

FROM ME TO YOU

I have a confession to make. I disliked history in school. I was not encouraged to read other than the textbooks, which were dreadfully dull.

Later, general reading about our country and its people made me realize how much I had missed. I regretted it deeply. This collection of stories has blossomed to make good for that regret, and I found that travelling back in time and peeping into the lives of queens and kings was amazingly interesting. The stories developed keeping the history line intact and adding embellishments to some. Dates and names are minimized, and certain chosen incidents from the maze of history are highlighted.

I wish you all happy reading.

I dedicate this book to my beloved motherland, India, for having nurtured brave-hearted queens and kings.

The same royalty I must thank for living their lives the way they did and enabling me to give an impressive shape to the stories. Of course, I thank the Hachette India team for helping me and you to enjoy writing and reading this book.

Indira Ananthakrishnan
Chennai, 2022

THE KINGS WHO STOPPED FIGHTING

One of the greatest civilizations recorded in Indian history flourished approximately two thousand years ago in south India. It consisted of the Chera, Chola and Pandya kingdoms. Despite many political conflicts, it was a period of immense economic prosperity and extraordinary literary activities. During this period, from time to time, Tamil scholars gathered in large numbers in congregations known as Sangams to present their literary works. Historians have called it the Sangam period in honour of these literary pursuits of that time. Many of the kings themselves were poets and patrons of art and culture. Besides kings, there were smaller but significant chieftains who also respected and supported the scholars. This story is based on a conflict between two chieftains, Athiyaman and Thondaiman, which would have resulted in war if not for the timely intervention of Avvaiyar, a scholar–poetess of that era.

King Athiyaman Neduman Anci, a great patron of art and literature, was seated on his throne. His son, Elini, sat to his right on a smaller seat. The décor of the royal court spelt richness in its simplicity, in keeping with the times – the Golden Age of the Sangam period, in the southern Thamizhagam province of the subcontinent.

The king surveyed the guests in his court. They came from different parts of the kingdom and some were from foreign lands. There were musicians, dancers and men and women who practised the literary arts. One by one, they came forward, paid their respects to the royal host and took their seats. The day was a special one for it marked the annual festival dedicated to music, dance and literature. Athiyaman looked forward to it every year and enjoyed it thoroughly. He took great pleasure in rewarding the artistes who pleased him with their skill and talent.

The performances began. Gorgeously dressed dancers glided gracefully onto the stage. The king and his son watched with wondrous joy. When the musicians performed, Athiyaman closed his eyes and listened in awe, his fingers keeping time with the rhythm of the music. Elini, on the other hand, did not appreciate music much. He quietly walked up to the dancers and talked to them in animated whispers.

At noon, the dance and music performance came to an end. Athiyaman thanked the artistes and bestowed them with generous gifts.

The afternoon was dedicated to poetry. The best poets of the kingdom as well as those from the neighbouring kingdoms of Chera, Chola and Pandya dynasties were present.

'Aha...well said, well said!' The king expressed his appreciation from time to time as he listened to the poets with rapt attention. The hours wore away pleasantly and the sun was well on its way to the western horizon.

The last presentation of the day was that of the renowned poetess, Avvaiyar – a small-built, self-effacing, elderly lady. Athiyaman had heard a lot about her verses and was eager to hear her recite some of them. Avvaiyar admired the king not only for his kind and gentle disposition, and love of art and culture, but also for his heroism and valour. Bowing respectfully to the stately figure seated on the throne, she began reciting in a rich tone of voice, sincere and devoid of flattery:

'The fame of our sunlike king
White and cool as the moon,
Will not blacken
Will not die.
If he has a little rice
He shares it in many plates,
And wherever spears and arrows fly, he is there
To spell victory.'

The king waited for her to continue, but just then, his chief minister walked in, looking worried and bowed deeply. A hush fell over those present.

The king frowned and asked with mounting irritation, 'Do you wish to disturb the court to announce some exceptional good tidings, Minister?'

'I am sorry to say the tidings are not good, Your Majesty,' replied the minster. 'I have news that King Thondaiman has sworn to attack our kingdom and has sent a message to that effect.'

Everyone gasped except the king.

'What now, Father?' Elini asked in a shaky voice.

'Well, son. We are not new to war. I have won many battles. Defeating Thondaiman will not be difficult,' he said complacently. He turned to the minister and said, 'Ask the commander-in-chief to prepare for war.'

One by one, the poets left the court loaded with gifts. Only Avvaiyar lingered. The king cast her a questioning look.

'As the most prized artiste of the day, I have given my most precious possession – my three-stranded pearl necklace. Does that not satisfy you?' he asked gently.

'I linger on for a different reason, Your Majesty,' Avvaiyar replied.

'And what is that?'

'I praised Your Majesty's heroism in my poem. Many a battle you have won. But there comes a time in life when peace is preferred to war,' Avvaiyar said boldly.

The king smiled and remarked, 'I take you for an esteemed poetess, not a warrior. Do you want to advise me on war and peace now?'

Avvaiyar brushed aside the king's taunt. The need of the hour was to avert a clash of arms, she said to herself and repeated in a stronger tone, 'Make peace, not war, Your Majesty.'

The king laughed aloud. 'In that case, I appoint you as my ambassador of peace to the court of King Thondaiman.'

'What can Avvaiyar do, Father?' Elini intervened, expressing his doubts about the arrangement. A flicker of hesitation passed over Avvaiyar's countenance, but she promptly brushed it aside and nodded – she was ready to go.

Early next morning, Avvaiyar set out for Thondaiman's kingdom.

Thondaiman welcomed Avvaiyar with great pleasure. The poetess was well known to him.

'It is my good fortune to have you here today,' he said to her.

'I was invited by King Athiyaman to recite in his court. Before leaving this area, I wished to see you also,' she informed him.

Avvaiyar was served a sumptuous lunch, after which Thondaiman said, 'If you are well rested, I would like

to take you to my weapons room.' He was very sure that she would be reporting all that happened in his court to Athiyaman.

King Thondaiman proudly showed her the array of armaments that were displayed there. Avvaiyar viewed them in speechless wonder.

Beaming with pride, King Thondaiman asked his guest, 'Well...what do you say? Don't you think Athiyaman will lose if I attack him?'

A couple of minutes passed in heavy silence. Then, Avvaiyar burst forth in poetic splendour:

'Maybe so, if you say so...
But Athiyaman's weapons are war-worn,
And his armour bloodstained
Being reborn, getting repaired,
Through skilled hands with utmost care...'

Avvaiyar paused and prayed silently for Thondaiman to understand the meaning of her words and recognize Athiyaman's superiority. He looked at her thoughtfully for a moment. The look then turned into a piercing one and he frowned.

As moments ticked on, Avvaiyar saw a change coming over him. He was drained of his pride.

'Yes, yes,' he said, nodding gravely. 'Athiyaman has fought many battles and won them too. I...I think

I would stand no chance against such a great warrior. Maybe, I should call off the war and choose peace.'

Avvaiyar breathed a sigh of relief.

Thondaiman wasted no time in accompanying Avvaiyar to Athiyaman's kingdom. When the two appeared in Athiyaman's court, the king was thunderstruck to see Thondaiman. He was not prepared to welcome an enemy who had declared war on him. He looked daggers at him. His right hand was ready to unsheathe his sword and his left hand was trembling in fury. Avvaiyar stepped back and watched the two kings in silence.

Before Athiyaman could do anything, Thondaiman came forward to pledge peace. 'King Athiyaman,' he said, 'I withdraw my declaration to wage war.'

Athiyaman was dumbfounded. 'Can this be true?' he asked himself. His hands fell limply to his side and Avvaiyar's words echoed in his mind. *There comes a time in life…*

His expression lost its fury and Thondaiman continued, 'Let our kingdoms be friendly and flourish in peace and harmony. This will be good for one and all.' The pause that followed was not an unfriendly one.

Athiyaman simply said, 'I agree.'

Elini was witness to the amazing change that came over his father thereafter. The king began to devote his time to the welfare of his subjects. He built more waterways and roadways, and beautified the towns and countryside. Elini supported his father in all his activities.

Athiyaman advised him, 'Remember to be friendly, my son. It pays better dividends than enmity. Weapons may be wielded only to defend oneself or to ensure the safety of our people.'

Athiyaman gave a special gift to Avvaiyar, a black *nellikai*, or Indian gooseberry, which was supposed to grant a long life to the receiver. Avvaiyar lived for many years, to sings her songs and delight the hearts of kings and subjects all over Tamizhagam, the place we call Tamil Nadu today. Avvaiyar wrote many verses in praise of Athiyaman, especially after he chose peace over war. In one such poem she said:

'He fought only when he was forced to,
If he had plenty, he shared with us,
If there was less, he gave up his share.
He accompanied us on the path of love,
But walked alone on the path of war.'

THE IN-BETWEEN KING

Not much is known about the life of King Bindusara, the second ruler of the Mauryan dynasty. His life story has been overshadowed by that of his father, Chandragupta, who was the founder of the great Mauryan dynasty, and that of his son, Ashoka, who was one of the greatest rulers in Indian history. Moreover, his period of rule has not been recorded in as much detail as the reigns of Chandragupta or Ashoka. Certain common accounts of Bindusara's life are found in Jain and Buddhist legends from the ancient and medieval times, although the versions are different. Besides, these were supposedly recorded much after his lifetime. Some of these extraordinary events that shaped his life have helped to give the story its form.

The baby was tiny and delicate, born seven days before it was due. The wet nurse held him gently in her hands. She fed him patiently with a small silver spoon. He swallowed the lukewarm milk, half a spoon at a time. Chanakya – friend, philosopher and guide of the Mauryan royal family – stood at a distance and watched.

The baby had his fill and fell asleep. He was kept in a special chamber that protected him from pollutants and possible infections. Chanakya relaxed when he saw the nurse cover him with a gossamer-thin blanket and leave the room noiselessly.

Things were tense for the next few days in the palace of King Chandragupta Maurya. His son was far too weak to be breast-fed or cuddled. The infant's chances of survival looked bleak. It wasn't until the baby began to gain weight and grow did the members of the palace breathe easy. Chanakya kept a close watch on the growing child, and the royal nurse looked after him well.

One day, when Bindusara was a toddler, he was playing in the palace garden with his friends, sons of the king's ministers. They were older than the prince and at times bullied him. So, the nurse kept a careful watch over them during playtime. While playing, Bindusara fell and started crying. One of the boys said to the others, 'You know, Bindu does not have a real mother to console him.'

Bindusara did not understand. He thought the nurse was his mother. Just then, the nurse went into the garden and said to him gently, 'Look at the lovely peacocks, Bindu. It is about to rain, and they are all set to dance. The *mayur* is the favourite animal of the Maurya clan, you know. They love to roam around in our garden.'

The toddler's attention turned to the peacock, and he forgot about his friend's remark.

Suddenly, it began to drizzle. The nurse asked the boys to run in. 'Let's see if the evening rain can wash away the blue spot on Bindu's forehead,' said another boy.

Bindu rubbed his forehead.

'Never mind that now. Just come inside,' said the nurse. 'That spot is a special mark,' she added as she picked up Bindu in her arms. 'Minister Chanakya chose the name Bindusara for him especially because of this spot. Do you know what it means, Bindu?

Bindu shook his head.

'It means "spot on the fair forehead".'

Bindusara smiled. He felt proud of his name and his birthmark.

The days rolled by. Bindusara learnt the art of warfare from Chanakya and other skilled warriors. His father had his hands full fighting the powerful Nandas of Magadha. He had little time to spend with his son, although he was keen to be with him and teach him about the Mauryan Empire. The boy too missed his father's company.

One morning, Bindusara spotted his father at a distance in a serious discussion with Chanakya. Bindusara wanted to run to him and started throwing a tantrum at breakfast.

'I just want to greet him before he goes away,' he said.

'Eat and then you may go. I won't stop you,' said his nurse and put the plate of khichri, topped with fried cashew nuts, in front of him. The child was in a hurry. He grabbed a handful from the centre of the plate, but dropped it immediately.

'Ouch! It's so hot!' he cried.

'Silly boy,' remarked the nurse, raising her voice. 'A plateful of freshly cooked food is always hot in the middle. You should always start eating from the sides.'

The wind carried these words to Chanakya's ears. He broke into a smile. He addressed Chandragupta, his heart racing with excitement, 'Your Majesty,' he said, 'I think a practical strategy to deal with our neighbours would be to attack the outermost parts of the region first. Then, we can gradually move to the centre.' Chandragupta nodded thoughtfully. He knew that Chanakya's ideas were always good. Little did he know that, this time, it was Bindusara's action that gave him the idea!

The Mauryan army lost no time in attacking and capturing the remote areas of the Nanda Empire. Winning them was easy; just the way Bindusara found it easy to eat the hot food first from the sides. Steadily, the army moved into 'the hottest part' at the centre. Here, it was a fierce battle. The Nandas put up a forceful fight for a considerable amount of time, but eventually lost. The Mauryan chariots victoriously thundered across the battlefield with their white banners fluttering high.

Chandragupta continued to make extensive conquests. The empire expanded to cover a large part of the subcontinent, and the king's fame spread far and wide. But then something happened that changed the course of history. Chandragupta, who thought of nothing else but defeating his neighbours and conquering lands, began to think differently. He was in his forties when this change came upon him. He called Bindusara and ceremoniously placed his glittering crown on his head. Bindusara was taken aback. He had not expected this. Speechless, he simply stared at his father.

'My son,' said Chandragupta. 'I want you to take charge of our kingdom. I have faith in you. And you have a strong counsellor in Chanakya. Always heed his advice. He will make sure that our dynasty endures.'

'And what about you...' Bindusara's voice trailed off.

Chandragupta smiled and said, 'Don't worry about me. I have the vast forest lands of our kingdom where I shall live peacefully, following in the footsteps of Lord Buddha.'

Bindusara assured his father, saying, 'You have also given me the name "Amitraghata", which means "destroyer of foes". Well, I will make sure I live up to it.' And so, Chandragupta renounced the throne and moved to a faraway part of the kingdom where he lived out his life as a Buddhist monk.

Ruling over the huge Mauryan Empire was no easy task for Bindusara. However, with power and foresight, he soon became the master of the entire territory between the Bay of Bengal in the east and the Arabian Sea in the west, as well as the area around the Indus Valley and the Gangetic plains. Chanakya felt proud of Bindusara's achievements. However, every time he saw the mark on Bindusara's forehead, a chill ran down his spine.

When Bindusara's wife gave birth to a son, she exclaimed in joy, 'I'm now without sorrow.' She turned at her husband and said, 'Let's call him Ashoka, the one "without sorrow".'

Bindusara, on the other hand, looked at his son with a frown. 'Hmm…' he sighed. 'He's not very handsome, is he?'

His wife was cut up by his remark. 'I did not expect these words from you. My son will take the legacy of the Mauryan dynasty to greater heights, you'll see,' she said haughtily and walked away with the baby in her arms.

Ashoka grew up to be an incredibly impressive and stately prince. His looks no longer mattered. Bindusara was awed by his skills. In fact, Ashoka became so powerful that he stole the limelight from his father. Soon, the reins of the kingdom were transferred to him. Bindusara retired and watched the Mauryan Empire expand and flourish under his son.

On a quiet evening, Bindusara and his wife were spending time in the moonlit peacock garden. They were rocking themselves in the golden swing when a shadowy figure appeared at the far end. It was slowly approaching the royal couple.

'Who's that?' Bindusara raised his voice. The queen held on to his hand.

'Chanakya,' came the reply.

'Come, come, Minister,' Bindusara welcomed him. 'I don't see much of you these days.'

'Yes... Your Highness, I would like to take leave of you and move away,' said Chanakya. His voice was feeble and his gait slow.

'What?' Bindusara was surprised. 'No. No one can take you away from the Mauryan kingdom.'

'Except the Almighty, my lord. His call has come. I don't have long to live. I'd like to live the remaining years of my life as a Buddhist monk, like your father, and pass this world with the Great Master in my mind,' replied Chanakya.

'I see. Well, I know I cannot stop you. I can only bid you a fond farewell,' said Bindusara softly.

'Thank you, Your Highness. However, I can't join the holy order without telling you the dark secret that's been weighing on my heart. I have a confession to make.'

The swing rocked as the startled couple sat up and waited for Chanakya to continue. The moon hid behind the clouds as if she did not want to hear what Chanakya would say.

'Let me take you back to the day you were born, Your Majesty.'

He then held up the magnificent Grecian urn he was holding. 'This beautiful urn was a present from your grandfather from Greece.'

'I don't understand,' Bindusara interrupted.

'My king, your mother was Greek. Your father had political ties with the Hellenic Empire. That was how he met your mother and fell in love with her.

'There used to be an elegant marble table on which this urn used to be kept. It served as a dinner table on special occasions when your parents wanted to spend some quiet time together. A week before you were born, your mother expressed her wish to eat at this table. As a pregnant woman's wishes are always fulfilled, your father readily agreed.

'A special dinner was cooked, and the table was laid. I saw to it that everything was right and then left them alone. Your mother, the queen, looked so elegant that day.

'Your parents clinked their glasses of wine and took a sip each. Then, your mother playfully plucked your father's cup from his hand and gave hers to him. Laughing, she gulped down the drink.

'I was shocked. Her action was so sudden...I couldn't stop her...' sighed Chanakya.

'But why did you want to stop her?' asked Bindusara, wondering where the story was going.

Chanakya sighed heavily and said, 'Let me explain. You see, it had been my habit to regularly mix a few drops of poison in your father's wine...'

Bindusara and his wife gasped.

'... Only because I wanted him to develop resistance to it. He had so many enemies – I had to make sure he was well protected.' Chanakya wiped a tear that wet the wrinkled corner of his eye and added, 'Your mother became unconscious and fell down instantly. I ran to her side. I knew the poison would kill her soon. You were in her womb, just seven days away from coming into the world.'

Bindusara's wife buried her face in his chest and whimpered.

'There was no time to waste.' Chanakya's voice was hoarse with sorrow as he continued. 'In a wink, I cut open her stomach and pulled you out. I did what was needed to make sure you lived.

'Pardon me, Your Majesty. I had no choice. I believe that the mark on your forehead is an effect of that poison.'

Not a sound could be heard in the garden. Even the night owl had stopped hooting.

Bindusara took a few heavy moments to respond. Deeply moved, he said, 'You are a saviour, my dear minister. I forgive you for your actions. What matters is that your intentions were noble and your heart was in the right place. The Mauryan Empire wouldn't have been what it is today if not for you.'

Without a word, Chanakya bowed deeply, turned and disappeared into the darkness.

THE AWESOME PALLAVAS

One of the greatest but historically lesser known dynasties that flourished in south India around 1,500 years ago was the Pallava dynasty. To this day, the Pallavas are renowned for their architectural genius. Their magnificent temples and structures cut out of colossal rock masses have survived through the centuries. Those on the southern shores of the Bay of Bengal at Mamallapuram or Mahabalipuram are a great tourist attraction today.

Despite wars, they never stopped their building activities. There was at least one major temple in every village and town. Many of these exist even today. A few historians, especially from the south, have recorded the story of the Pallavas in great detail.

The Pallava king Mahendravarman I was a warrior, administrator, author, artist and musician , all wrapped in one kingly figure. He had undertaken a unique project and was obsessed with it.

One day, he rode in his royal chariot towards the seashore to supervise the launch of the project. It was a two-hour ride from his palace to the sea. All along the way, he visualized caves excavated out of the granite hills that stood like dark giants on the seashore. The caves would house sculptures and paintings of deities.

The steeds galloped faster than the early morning wind that blew from the sea. The king's attention was drawn to the sound of waves when the chariot came to a halt. His chief sculptor, the *maha-sthapathi,* and his fellow workers, the *thachchar*s, were waiting for him.

The king hopped out of the chariot, excited like a child. He surveyed the sandy expanse dotted with tall palm trees and big boulders. The sun was already heating up. He was glad to be wearing fine, white cotton clothes with just a bejewelled turban and a simple, long gold chain to go with it.

The *sthapathi* took the king around the site, explaining to him how the shrines and sculptures would be designed.

'Our workers have agreed to work on this project. The outcome of their labour along with your ardent support and the blessings of Vishwakarma, the heavenly lord of architects, will make this shoreline a great attraction that will be remembered for many years to come!'

The king was pleased. 'You may start work,' he told the *sthapathi*. 'I will not be able to come often to see the progress. I will send you my suggestions from time to time through my messenger.'

The king then distributed baskets of thirst-quenching palm fruit to the workers. A large earthen pot of salted buttermilk, flavoured with ginger and curry leaves, was also unloaded from the chariot and placed in the shade of a boulder. The workers thanked the king for his thoughtful gesture. The chariot then carried the king back to the palace in the capital city of Kanchi.

Work went on steadily at the seashore. It was hard labour. Unmindful of the scorching sun or the warm breeze, the rock cutters and sculptors worked sincerely from early morning to late evening, shaping the rocks as per the king's wishes.

After a few days, when the king visited the site, he found the rock-cut temples taking shape. He was delighted! He told the chief sculptor, 'I have confidence in your expertise and the skill of the workers. Continue working at your pace, *sthapathi*. There is no hurry.' With these words of encouragement, the king went back.

Life was not all about art and architecture for the Pallava king, though. Very soon, Mahendravarman had to face an attack from his neighbour, Pulakeshin II of the Chalukya kingdom, who was keen on capturing the Pallava kingdom. Pulakeshin had advanced as far as the prized city of Kanchi and there was an intense, pitched battle, with both armies colliding fiercely just outside the city. The battle lasted for several days and many lives were lost. Mahendravarman managed to stop Pulakeshin from entering Kanchi, but he lost the northern provinces of his kingdom to the Chalukyas.

Narasimhavarman, the son of Mahendravarman and the next Pallava king, swore to avenge his father's defeat. While he was biding his time to attack the Chalukyas, his attention was drawn to the rock-cut temples that his father had initiated. Narasimhavarman too was a notable patron of art and culture. He wanted to introduce new styles of architecture in the temples, and so he decided to take time off from his administrative duties to visit the work site.

The next morning, the king was up early for his wrestling exercise. He then had a refreshing bath in the royal pool. That morning, he did not wear his usual ceremonial clothes. Instead, he wore a plain white dhoti of fine cotton around his waist. A finer cloth, with a border delicately woven in gold, was loosely thrown over his shoulder to cover the upper part of his body. He wore his jewelled crown and a chain of gold round his neck once he had offered prayers at the palace temple. Relishing a hot drink of coffee made from freshly roasted and ground coffee powder, he waited for the *maha-sthapathi* to arrive.

The sculptor came just as the clock tower chimed six. Then, the king and he walked briskly towards the stables. Two stately steeds trotted up to them, drawing the royal chariot. The men climbed in and at the charioteer's signal, the horses broke into a quick trot. Once they left the palace grounds, they sped towards the seashore.

Mahendravarman had fondly named his dream project Mamallapuram. *Ma-malla* meant great wrestler, and when he saw his youthful son growing into a strong wrestler, he decided to name it so in his honour.

On reaching Mamallapuram, Narasimhavarman was astounded. He remembered his father and thanked him for having conceived the architectural wonder that lay before him. He promised himself to add more beauty to it.

Suddenly, he noticed a huge boulder that was still untouched, and an idea came to him in a flash. He told the chief sculptor, 'This could be a beautiful cave temple for Devi Durga. While the main shrine can be inside the cave, the side walls could display carved panels of…' Before the king could finish expressing his thoughts, the sculptor added his own, excitedly,

'Yes, Your Majesty! Durga mounted on a lion wielding various weapons in her eight arms against the demon Mahishasura.'

'Excellent! And the other panel can have Vishnu reclining serenely on the coils of the snake, Adishesha.'

The sculptor nodded enthusiastically.

'Go ahead, then. Now I must get back to my work. My ministers are waiting for me.'

Off went the royal chariot back to the palace. The king hastened to the audience hall where the ministers had assembled to discuss state matters with him. Among other things, the war minister reminded the king, 'Your Majesty, you have long been expressing your wish to avenge your father's defeat. Should we prepare to go to war with Pulakeshin?'

'Yes, it is time. Let us get started right away,' replied Narasimhavarman.

The rest of the day was given up to administrative work and courtly duties. The king remained busy with dictating letters and entertaining some visiting dignitaries. Evening was the only time he could relax when he and the royal family attended performances in the audience hall. The queen could not meet him till after the cultural programme gave over, late in the evening.

Before retiring for the night, the queen asked the king when he would take her to visit the rock temples.

'Any time you wish, my dear. But my priority right now is our impending war against the Chalukya king. Once I have defeated him, we will pay a visit to Devi Durga and thank her.'

The war against the Chalukyas was a long-drawn-out one. Both the armies were equally strong. Remembering his father, Narasimha fought with single-minded determination to win. He won back the lands his father had lost and drove the enemy away for good.

He then went to war against the neighbouring Chola, Chera and Pandya kings, and defeated them too. The Pallava kingdom expanded, and Narasimha earned the title of Empire Builder.

Even with all of this going on, Mamallapuram was not forgotten. The king was waiting for a respite to visit it. After the wars, when the damaged towns were repaired and the warriors amply compensated, the king was ready to visit the shore temple. He had not forgotten the promise he had made to his wife either.

'We'll leave in the afternoon when the sun is not too strong and return before dark,' he told her.

The queen was excited. She wore a flowing garment of finely spun silk, a chest band with a delicate silver border and an upper garment thrown over the shoulder like a stole. Her hair was tied up and adorned with strings of pearls and fragrant jasmine flowers. The king admired her long earrings,

gold armlets, bangles, necklace and a waistband studded with gems.

The cave temple of Goddess Durga left the queen spellbound. She pinched herself to make sure that she was not dreaming. Not only did she offer prayers, along with flowers and fruit, to the Goddess but also donated generously from her personal wealth for the continued upkeep of the temple.

The cluster of five richly sculpted rathas, each carved out of a single rock, resembling temple chariots, was being given the final touches now. The king and queen could not take their eyes off the ornamented towers and the decorative niches that displayed intricately carved figures of deities, dancers and a host of other creatures.

'Look,' said the queen pointing to another granite hillock nearby. There were groups of monkeys and elephants carved on it.

The king laughed. 'Our people have a soft corner for animals, you know.'

The *sthapathi* then showed them a carved image of the king standing majestically with his hands on his hips.

'That's you!' exclaimed the queen. It was a surprise for the king too. He had not commissioned it. He congratulated the sculptors for their wonderful work and showered them with gifts. The sun was setting when Narasimhavarman and his queen rode back home.

When it was dark, the king and his chief minister disguised themselves as common men and went into the city. They walked the roads at a leisurely pace. They went past houses, markets, temples, Buddhist monasteries and Jain shrines. The kingdom was alive with talk and activities in the late evening hour. The king could feel the joys as well as the grievances of his people. Their joys made him happy. Their grievances he vowed to set right.

Three decades later, the Pallava kingdom had metamorphosed into a magically serene and peaceful one. It was the reign of King Rajasimha, the great-grandson of Narasimhavarman.

King Rajasimha made further enhancements to the temples and rock structures. He designed and constructed another magnificent temple at Mamallapuram, built from a huge stone block. The temple was so close to the sea that the waves continually broke against its walls. It came to be known as the Shore Temple. Sculpted on its walls were large, breathtaking figures of gods and goddesses, village scenes and events from mythological tales.

By this time, Mamallapuram had developed into a large port city that lay to the north of the splendid shore temples and cave shrines. Ships frequently sailed in and out of the harbour, carrying traders and travellers to and from distant lands. The deep waters were dangerous and made it difficult for ships to sail smoothly when the nights were dark.

Realizing this, the king decided to get a lighthouse built. It was a stately tower built on top of a temple that stood on a hillock. Right at the building's pinnacle was the lantern room with glass windows. It housed an immense lamp with a wick made with several yards of cloth. It was lit using huge quantities of oil, and its beacon was visible for many miles into the sea to help guide ships towards a safe harbour.

The last of the awesome Pallavas was Nandivarman. When he ascended the throne, the kingdom had reached the zenith of richness. The kings of the surrounding kingdoms were eyeing it.

The Chalukya king Vikramaditya ll marched with his powerful army into the realm of the Pallavas. He captured the outlying regions and advanced to the capital, Kanchi. The sight of Kanchi left Vikramaditya spellbound. He was overwhelmed by grandeur of the city – the broad avenues, the magnificent palace, the mansions and, above all, the majestic temples with their lifelike sculptures. He did not have the heart to destroy its beauty. War ceased and he set about renovating the city of Kanchi and repairing the damage it had suffered. The restored city looked even more beautiful than before. He let the Pallavas live peacefully in it and marched back homewards vowing to make his own Chalukya capital as mesmerizing as Kanchi.

Nandivarman was amazed by the change that came over Vikramaditya. He thanked the deity at the temple of Kailasanatha in Kanchi and the entire kingdom celebrated.

After Nandivarman, there were three more kings who ruled the Pallava kingdom. But they struggled to hold on to their dominion. Large parts of it were steadily lost in the next few decades until, at last, the Chola and Pandya kings took over the entire kingdom. Thus ended the once glorious reign of the awesome Pallavas.

THE KING OF KINGS

The Chola king Arulmozhi Varman reigned over a large part of south India at the turn of the 11th century. History declares him as the greatest Chola emperor – the King of Kings (or Rajaraja) and he reigned as lord paramount for more than two decades. Apart from good governance, he excelled in promoting architecture, art and literature. He maintained an official record of his rule to inspire future generations. Constructed under his patronage, the Brihadisvara Temple is the epitome of architectural excellence. Visitors to the temple today are amazed to see how it has stood the test of time for over a thousand years. Rajaraja Chola was also known for his humility and compassion.

The Chola Empire at the time of Arulmozhi's birth was a powerful and expanding one. The kingdom rejoiced at the birth of this lovely child whose name meant 'blessed with wisdom'. However, no one thought he would become the king because he was fourth in the line of accession to the throne.

Arulmozhi grew up to be a charming prince – strong, confident and adventurous. His father sent him out on several political campaigns, and he came back successful every time. The prince did not aspire to be the king, but a series of rival claims ended in his wearing the crown. Soon, Arulmozhi proved himself to be a great king in every sense of the word.

The king's subjects would often praise their monarch and his way of ruling the kingdom.

'Our king is wise and kind, just as his name suggests, but he has proved to be much more than that,' said one man to his friends as they sat sipping tea.

'Oh, yes! No doubt about it,' chimed in another man.

'A brave warrior…' said a third.

'He's given us a life of joy. The comfortable houses we live in, the beautiful gardens, the irrigation system that is a boon to farmers – such a good idea of his, isn't it?'

'An intelligent administrator… Has a heart of gold…' on and on they went, extolling Arulmozhi's many virtues.

'Is there anybody who has a different opinion?' asked a bold young man with a loud voice. Everyone shook their heads.

'In that case, henceforth, our beloved king should be known as Rajaraja, the King of Kings!' he declared in a louder tone.

'Hear! Hear!' the men yelled in approval.

'Not just Rajaraja. He's Rajaraja Chola!' an elderly lady added. 'We are proud of our king and our kingdom.' Applause and joyful shouts echoed in the air.

After that day, the name Arulmozhi Varman was rarely used. The king was Rajaraja Chola to his subjects, to the country and to the world.

Rajaraja Chola was extremely restless. He had been tense and ill at ease all day, waiting for the return of his commander-in-chief from the battlefield. So far during his reign, he had fought several fierce battles and won them all. Thus, his empire had expanded steadily. But this time, it was different. He was fighting against the Pandya army, a powerful military force that was as strong as his own army. Even their war strategies were evenly matched.

The king paced the floor nervously. What news would his commander bring? Good or bad? He prayed to Lord Shiva, the family deity to whom he was deeply devoted.

Finally, at sundown, the commander-in-chief came with news of victory. Tears of joy flowed down

Rajaraja's cheeks. He took several deep breaths. The bells of the palace temple chimed in time for the evening prayers. The king turned around to face the direction of the temple, folded his hands high above his head and chanted 'Om Namah Shivaya!' thrice. Celebrations of the victory would have to wait till the morning. Rajaraja retired to his chamber; the day had been exhausting, to say the least. The chambermaid brought him a glass of warm milk flavoured with *khus* and almonds. As he sipped it, he grew thoughtful.

'Battle upon battle, victory after victory... But is that all there is to life?' he muttered. Just then, Kundavai, his older sister entered his chamber.

'Come, Akka,' he said, brightening up a little. He had great respect and affection for her. She was esteemed in the family for her keen intelligence and learning.

'What's the matter, Thambi? You look troubled,' she asked with sisterly concern.

'I was just thinking... Is victory in war my only accomplishment? Surely, I should be doing more... Other greater things!'

Kundavai raised her eyebrows. 'But my dear brother, you are already doing so much for your people. There is not a soul that is unhappy.'

'As always, you're right, Akka. When I visit my people disguised as one of them, I do find them happy and content, but...'

'But what, Thambi?'

'I want to do something that will immortalize the Chola Empire...'

Kundavai was speechless. However, she was aware she had to say something. Her brother depended on her counsel.

'Let's give it a good thought. Tomorrow, after the celebrations are over, we can talk about this. Now come, let's go and have dinner.'

'No, Akka. My head aches. I'd rather go to sleep.'

'The poor boy! The stress of the battle has gotten to him,' she said to herself and wished him good night.

The temple bells chimed again. It was time for the shrine to be closed for worship. The sound of the bells resonated in Rajaraja's ears. He rubbed his forehead, and just like that, the headache was gone, and an idea began to form in his mind.

'I must talk this over with my sister in the morning,' he said to himself, barely able to contain his excitement. Moments later, he fell into a deep slumber.

In the morning, the preparations for the celebration began with gusto. The king waited impatiently for it to be over. All he could think about was discussing his idea with Kundavai. Finally, when they were alone, he said to her with great enthusiasm, 'Akka, I want to build a temple.'

Kundavai did not seem impressed. There was a moment of awkward silence, after which she said, 'Well, my dear Thambi, our kingdom is full of temples. Why do you want to add one more to the count?'

Rajaraja replied, 'We'll build a different one. It will be colossal! A grand, impressive structure made of stubbornly strong, solid stone and granite. The idols of the deity Shiva and his bull Nandi will be gigantic! Can't you imagine it?'

Kundavi stared at her excited brother. 'I understand,' she murmured. 'Such a building will last forever. But how will you accomplish this feat?'

'I know it will be challenging, but we'll get the best of architects to begin with and work carefully on the plan. I hope I have your support, dear Akka,' he said decisively.

'I'm with you. You yourself are a brilliant self-taught architect and a supreme thinker. We'll do what we can. And remember, we have the great architect, Lord Shiva, himself dwelling in our hearts,' Kundavai said with sisterly affection. The king took her hands in his and pressed them gently.

In a few days, dark monsoon clouds covered the sky and there was rain. But that did not make the king sit back. He summoned the architects and worked with them indoors. The temple would be at the centre of the capital city of Thanjavur, laid out across a large area of about fifty acres. Everything was worked out with great precision and care down to the last detail.

Thanjavur was on the banks of the river Kaveri. The rainy season had begun, and the river was in spate. The people enjoyed her fullness and celebrated. The king and his planners, however, worked non-stop late into the nights, in an effort to finalize the plan.

After the rains ceased, thousands of workers were recruited. The best of artisans, stonecutters, sculptors, and other skilled and unskilled workers poured into the city. The farmers worked doubly hard to provide grain for all. The king ordered the masons to build comfortable *choultries* or resting places for the workers who came from far-off lands. He also ensured that they were provided with food and water. The weavers wove durable work clothes for them. Healers were alerted to be ready to treat the workers in case of accidents.

All the people – young and old, strong and weak, men and women – wanted to do whatever they could to help their beloved king in his venture. Work began to move fast. The king did not forget to thank the Almighty at every stage.

Where would the granite come from? A search party was sent to look for it and located a mine about 40 kilometres away from Thanjavur. The distance did not dishearten the king. The bullocks were well fed and fattened and carts were made sturdier than before. Within weeks, caravans of bullock carts loaded with granite were trooping into the city daily.

'What an ambitious project, my dear brother! But tell me, how you are going to raise the 80-tonne capstone and place it over the tall main tower?' asked Kundavai with concern.

The king laughed and said, 'I've discussed it in detail with my team of super thinkers. I wish you had been there at the meeting to give your suggestions. But you were, unfortunately, indisposed at that time.'

Kundavai waited for him to continue.

'My strongest-of-the-strong war elephants will help me out in this task. The workers have piled up a sandhill as high as the tower and placed big logs across it. The elephants will roll the stone along these logs and up the hill to reach the top of the main tower.'

'Well done!' exclaimed Kundavai. 'Remember the power of chanting during the lift. Our scriptures and our sages have proved its ability to help heavy objects levitate. Don't be in a hurry to finish this final step of the work. Even the slightest slip can be disastrous.'

The king drew a deep breath and nodded gravely. 'I understand, Akka,' he said softly.

Rajaraja spent a lot of time with the elephants to make sure they were in good health. Veterinary doctors examined them thoroughly. The king then disguised himself and mingled with the workers to find out if they were confident enough to undertake the colossal, back-breaking task. When he was totally satisfied, the work of raising the capstone began.

Chants started resonating in the air from before sunrise. At the most auspicious morning hour, the capstone started its upward journey. Time ticked on, hour after hour. Perspiration moistened the atmosphere. The sun journeyed up in the sky steadily and then began to set, feeling happy to sense the faith and confidence in the air. The elephants pushed the capstone up without a break. It was past sunset when the work was finally over. Surrounded by roaring cheers and tearing applause, the capstone stood majestically atop the main tower. Even the rising moon shed tears of joy.

The sculptors sculpted many days and nights to give Nandi, the giant bull, its awe-inspiring shape.

Then, the final preparations began for installing the main deity that matched the size of Nandi. A prayer ceremony was held in the sanctum sanctorum, the innermost chamber of the temple, to mark the occasion. Nandi was the only other witness apart from the priests and the royal family.

That night, the king slept soundly; as deeply as he slept on the day the idea of building the temple had crept into his mind.

The following day at sunrise, with the first chime of the enormous temple bell, the shrine would be thrown open for worship. But who would ring the temple bell? Quite obviously, the one who had truly worked for the construction of the temple, and that was the king.

Next morning, Rajaraja Chola pulled the cord of the bell and...the bell did not ring. Silence. Nothing

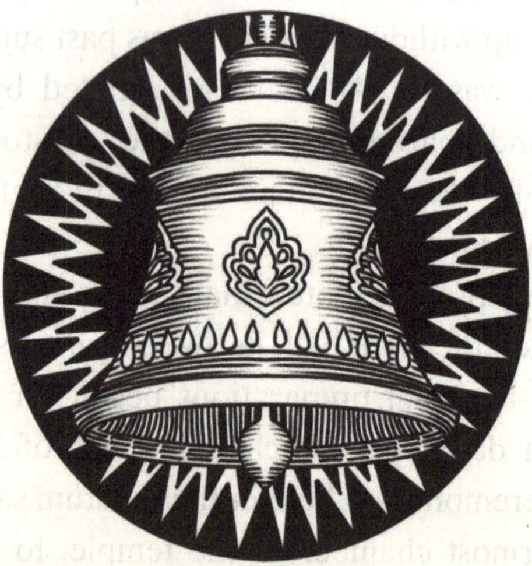

happened. Everyone else, starting from the high priest followed by the special Shiva devotees who chanted mantras, to the architects, engineers, skilled workers and other workers pulled the cord one after another. Still there was nothing. The rest of the people lined up to pull the cord, but the bell simply refused to make any sound.

The day dissolved into dusk and then to darkness. *Has something gone terribly wrong?* the king wondered.

The person at the end of the line was an old woman, wrinkled and frail. With folded hands she walked up to the bell and pulled the cord with all her strength. Instantly, the bell rang, the vibrations of its chimes reverberating in the darkness.

Everyone was amazed. No one moved or spoke. The king walked up in a daze to the old woman. He paid his respects to her and asked her humbly, 'May I know what your contribution to the temple construction has been?'

In a feeble, tremulous tone the woman replied that each day, she would stand by the highway from morning to night, come rain or shine, to supply water to the bullocks that carried the heavy slabs of granite from far-off places.

The king was taken aback. He had forgotten about providing water for the bullocks! Would Lord Shiva forgive him? Did he deserve the title King of Kings?

Questions cascaded in his mind until Kundavai came and gently shook him out of his stupor.

'Shiva is waiting for the puja. Let's not delay,' she said gently.

It was an all-night prayer. The kingdom rejoiced as never before while the king prayed gratefully to Shiva for making him aware of his neglect.

'Kingship is like riding the rough seas', he reminded himself. 'Being at the helm and steering the ship to safety is not an easy task.' He vowed to be more meticulous and conscientious than ever before, and he remembered that till the end of his life.

THE DANCING QUEEN

King Vishnuvardhana ruled over Hoysala in ancient Karnataka in the 12th century. His wife, Queen Shantala Devi, was known for her beauty, intelligence and proficiency in the dance form of Bharatanatyam and music. The king controlled the administrative system and Shantala supported him greatly. She used her skills to enhance the cultural and religious grandeur of the kingdom. She commissioned sculptors to create stunning female figurines in various Bharatanatyam dance poses for the Chennakesava temple at Belur and a few others. After her untimely death, King Vishnuvardhana built the Sri Shantaleswara Temple in her memory. Some features of these temples were lost in subsequent invasions. However, the structures are reasonably intact and attract tourists even today.

The rhythmic beat of '*thaiyum – taka – thaiyum – taka*' could be heard coming from a humble house at the far end of the street. The jingle of ankle bells kept time with the beats. It became fast when the beats went faster and slowed down when the beats became slower. This harmony went on tirelessly until one last beat marked the end of the activity. The jingling of anklets ceased.

'Well done, girls,' said an elderly voice. The house resounded with the laughter of two girls as they ran through its length. They were beautiful and dressed in brightly coloured long skirts and short blouses. They had identical hairstyles – two long plaits adorned with flowers. The girls sat down on the verandah and removed their ankle bells.

'See you tomorrow, girls. Don't forget to practise the steps. This is only the beginning. From here on, the steps will only get harder. And don't forget, you also need to master your mudras and bhavas. Only consistent practice with dedication can help you become exceptional Bharatanatyam dancers,' the tutor said, following them out into the verandah.

The girls jumped up excitedly and said, 'We are ready for all of it! We want to dance at the temple and receive the blessings of Chennakesava.'

The tutor smiled and left.

The house belonged to Marasinganaya, a general in the army of King Vishnuvardhana of the kingdom of Hoysala. The girls were his daughters, Shantala and Lakshmi. Right from the age of five, Shantala had dreamed of becoming a dancer. Lakshmi – her younger sister – too shared her ambition.

The girls practised till late that night and got up early in the morning to get ready for their dance lessons.

In the days that followed, the tutor taught them various aspects of the dance form and the music that accompanied the dance. It wasn't an easy task for either the tutor or the students. Finally, after many months of regular tutelage and consistent practice, the two teenagers were ready for the *arangetram* – their debut performance at the temple.

Dance costumes were stitched and matching jewellery and heavy, resounding ankle bells were bought for the girls. Their dresses were made using a brightly coloured silk with a golden border and were fashioned as saris with pleats that opened out like a fan. For easy leg movement, the dress tightened below the knees, somewhat like a pyjama. A tight blouse and a broad, ornamented belt at the waist accentuated the girls' slender figures. Their long braids were decorated not only with jasmine flowers but also jewelled headpieces. A bright red bindi at the centre of the forehead, eyes brightened with kohl and reddened lips were meant to draw attention to the bhavas or facial expressions. The mehendi on their hands and feet was meant to highlight the mudras or hand movements. They were bejewelled from top to toe. They wore armlets and bangles to match their dresses, dangling earrings, jewel-encrusted chokers and long golden chains around their necks. Each girl wore three rows of ankle bells on each foot, which would lend a resounding effect to the rhythmic footwork.

It was a full moon evening. Shantala and Lakshmi, dressed in all their dance finery, went to the temple with their parents and tutor. They paid obeisance to Lord Chennakesava, circumambulated the temple and then got on to the polished stone platform built within the temple premises for special religious and cultural performances. The tutor, with his wooden stick and beating block, sat at the right-hand corner of the platform. He was accompanied by a musician. The girls' parents sat down in the open space in front of the stage. Excited to see the performance, a huge crowd was already gathered there. The moon peeped out of the eastern horizon and quickly rose in the sky. Brighter than ever, the moon was competing with the glow of the oil lamps that lit the platform.

The performance began. Shantala and Lakshmi danced like two celestial nymphs. People watched with open-mouthed awe and wonder. They were so engrossed that no one noticed King Vishnuvardhana entering the temple.

The king of Hoysala was a devout Hindu. He had built the temple when he came to power, and he never failed to visit the temple on every full moon evening. As he entered, he looked up and admired the temple tower that stood over the entrance. It was an amazing piece of architecture. The tall pyramidal tower or gopuram towered over the entrance majestically. It was richly decorated with intricately carved figures of gods and goddesses, dancers and musicians as well as animals such as elephants, horses, cows, serpents and birds in various moods and forms. A long passage from the entrance led to the interior of the temple, up to the sanctum sanctorum. This passage had a lotus pond on one side and the stone platform with its surrounding open space on the other. During his visits, the king usually walked right through the passage with his attention focused on the sanctum sanctorum. But on this day, he could not move an inch beyond the passage. He was completely captivated by what was happening on the stage.

Have the heavens descended? Who are these heavenly dancers, he wondered. He could not take his eyes off the tall, graceful figure of Shantala. His heart beat feverishly fast. Only when the music and dance stopped did he gather his senses. He remembered that he had to move on to pay homage to the deity of the temple.

That night, the king did not sleep a wink. So far, he had not taken the matter of marriage seriously. Just the other day, his grandmother had tried to persuade him to think about it.

'You and your kingdom need a queen, my dear child. There are so many princesses eagerly waiting to be chosen as the queen of Hoysala. Why do you hesitate?'

Vishnuvardhana had responded, 'A king lives by the sword and dies by the sword.'

He further added, 'Hoysala has been constantly fighting with the neighbouring kingdoms of the Chalukyas and the Pallavas to prevent them from encroaching on our territory. Our earlier kings who have married and died on the battlefield have left behind only grieving widows. Should I do the same?'

But that night all of this dissolved into nothingness. He could not stop thinking about Shantala. He wanted her to be his queen.

When he expressed his wish to his grandmother, she was taken aback. Her grandson was ready to marry! Although relieved, she was unhappy about his choice.

'She's a mere general's daughter…she is no princess!' she exclaimed.

Vishnuvardhana turned a deaf ear to her protests. He would marry Shantala and none other. The royal family had no option. They decided to fulfil Vishnuvardhana's wish and approached Shantala and her parents to ask for her hand in marriage. Here, however, an unforeseen objection came from Shantala's side.

'I am a Jain by birth. Jainism is my religion. I respect Hinduism and accept it as a great religion. But I won't marry into a Hindu family and embrace Hinduism, even if it is royalty,' Shantala said. 'Moreover, I can't ever part with my sister. We will live together till the end of our lives.'

Vishnuvardhana was sore with disappointment. His heart had never been so heavy. But he was determined to make Shantala his queen. He looked into her eyes and said, 'I will not compel you to become a Hindu – you will have the freedom to retain your religion. If your sister means that much to you, she can come with you as well…as long as I get to spend my life with you.'

Shantala smiled and said, 'In that case, I willingly agree to be queen of Hoysala, but…'

Vishnuvardhana's heart sank. *What now?* he wondered.

Shantala continued, 'My ankle bells are a part of me. I promise to fulfil my duties as a queen, but I will not stop dancing.'

The king breathed a sigh of relief. 'Of course, you will not,' he said softly.

Vishnuvardhana and Shantala and Lakshmi were married at an auspicious hour on the appointed day. Hoysala had not witnessed a grander wedding. There was dancing and music besides all the festivities and feasts.

The joyous mood continued even after the wedding was over. Flowers danced to the music in the air. There was rhythm in everyone's movements.

Vishnuvardhan felt as though he was the most fortunate king in the history of the dynasty. Shantala was greatly interested in matters of administration and proved an able adviser to the king. She wasn't happy simply sitting on the throne. She travelled the length and breadth of the kingdom to get to know her subjects and understand their concerns. The people of the kingdom were delighted to meet their queen and poured their hearts out to her.

News about Hoysala's queen spread to the neighbouring kingdoms. The Chalukya king was curious to see this great queen that everyone was talking about.

'Making a friendly visit to Hoysala is out of question. The two kingdoms have never been on good terms. What shall I do?' the Chalukya king asked his minister.

'Declare war,' the minister suggested.

The king looked puzzled.

The minister smiled and said, 'They say that every time Vishnuvardhana prepares for war, Queen Shantala dances at the Chennakesava temple to seek the deity's blessings for victory. Once you declare war…'

'…the queen will perform at the temple,' said the king, catching the drift of the minister's words.

'Could you not sneak into the temple in disguise and watch her dance? You…'

The king did not let the minister finish. He jumped up from his seat and cried, 'Excellent idea! Declare war.'

Even before the sun set, the Chalukya war drummers began to beat their drums loudly.

Vishnuvardhana was upset.

'Why now when everyone is so happy and content?' he muttered.

Shantala pacified him. 'Can a kingdom live without war? We have Lord Chennakesava to protect us. You offer your prayers to him before you go to the battlefield, and I will dance for him to grant you victory.'

And so, thc following morning, Vishnuvardhana got ready to leave for the battlefield.

That evening, the temple was packed with spectators while Shantala and Lakshmi performed a special dance dedicated to Lord Chennakesava. When the performance was at its height and everyone was engrossed in watching it, in walked two men in plain clothes. They blended in with the crowd and quickly took their seats but not before being spotted by Shantala's sharp eyes. She almost missed a step when she saw them.

Those men don't look like natives... Who are they? she wondered. She plucked out the disturbing thought from her mind and turned her focus back to her dance.

'I am dancing for the Lord and for the king's victory,' she reminded herself.

After the performance, she caught a glimpse of the two figures slipping out of the temple while the rest of the crowd was still applauding.

In the morning, Vishnuvardhana bade farewell to Shantala and Lakshmi, and led the army for war. But then, the strangest thing happened. Even before Vishnuvardhana could reach the battlefield, he was informed that the Chalukya king had declared peace and withdrawn his army.

Vishnuvardhana was astonished, but Shantala was not. She laughed and remarked mysteriously, 'I guessed as much.'

Vishnuvardhana was speechless. He waited for her to explain.

Shantala continued, 'Last evening during the dance performance, two strangers sneaked into the audience. No one noticed, but I saw them. I am sure it was the Chalukya king and his companion in disguise. They had no intention of fighting. I think they just wanted to enjoy the dance. Their wish fulfilled, they withdrew.'

She took her husband's hands in hers and said affectionately, 'I know you missed a chance to fight and win. But we must thank Lord Chennakesava for averting the war and loss of lives.'

'And I must thank you too,' Vishnuvardhana added gratefully.

The Pandya king's intentions, however, were not as harmless as that of the Chalukya monarch. He wanted to make Hoysala a part of his kingdom, and so he declared war.

Soon enough, Vishnuvardhana had to rush to the battlefield – this time for real. At the same time, Shantala danced at the temple with great faith.

Vishnuvardhana won the war. He drove the Pandya forces out of his territory. The kingdom of Hoysala rejoiced.

'Hail to our dancing queen and victorious king,' they cheered.

Shantala decided to pay her tribute to Lord Chennakesava by beautifying the temple and its surrounding spaces by adding special structures. She built mandapas or porch-like structures leading to the shrines of gods and goddesses. These mandapas were adorned with sculptures. She saw to it that the pillars and ceilings of the mandapas were adorned with carvings of richly decorated figurines of dancing girls in various postures and of characters from the Puranas. The most talented sculptors in the kingdom were invited to carve out these magnificent figures. Although the figures were made of soapstone, their facial expressions and thoughtfully designed costumes looked all too real. The devotees who visited the temple were awestruck by its beauty and thanked Shantala for giving them such a delightfully divine experience.

Shantala had more temples constructed in and around the capital city of Belur. The sanctity of these temples increased the faith and fervour of the people and helped them to lead better lives.

However, every kingdom in any era has its share of woes, and Hoysala was no exception. Gloom descended upon the land when Shantala did not bear a child even after several years of marriage. Who would reign after Vishnuvardhana? She was the *pattamahadevi* or main queen. It did not matter if Lakshmi or the other queens had sons.

Shantala tried her best to persuade her husband to adopt Lakshmi's child as his heir, but he was firm in his refusal. She felt she had failed in fulfilling her duties as the queen of the dynasty.

Maybe if I am no longer in the king's life, it might help him to choose an heir, she thought. And so, with this thought in mind, Shantala quietly left the palace one evening, unnoticed by anyone.

Shantala wandered deep into the forest and walked a long way till she spotted a tall hill.

It was steep and the climb difficult, but she braved it with determination. Finally, Shantala reached the top with sore feet and lungs screaming for air. She took one look at the deep valley below and her heart missed a beat.

'Jump and you will be gone forever,' her mind urged.

But the very next moment, she heard another voice – it seemed to be coming from somewhere deep within. It questioned gently, 'But are you not a Jain? Does your faith permit you to take your life?'

Shantala shuddered as a nervous chill shook her body. Her resolve staggering, she stepped away from the edge, turned and began to walk with faltering steps. Monkeys chattered loudly as she plodded downhill and disappeared into the dense jungle. She lived out her last days there, following the Jain tradition of fasting unto death.

Vishnuvardhana was devastated after Shantala left the palace. There was no one in the royal household who could console him. Sometimes he would take long walks into the forest and sigh when he remembered the sounds of ankle bells that emanated from his queen's dancing feet. At other times, he would spend hours at the temples built by Shantala and see her in the figures of the dancers carved in stone. He assured himself that her spirit continued to live in Hoysala and felt comforted.

In the absence of a successor to the throne, the royal family worried about the future of the dynasty. *What would happen after Vishnuvardhana?* they wondered. Little did they know that the king too was plagued by the thought.

'The glory of the Hoysalas has to live on,' Shantala's persuasive voice whispered in Vishnuvardhana's heart. It made him choose a worthy heir who continued to uphold the honour of Hoysala for several years after him.

Eventually, there came a time when the magnificence of the dynasty began to fade. The Hoysala kings who came later could no longer hold their own against invaders who destroyed the glory of the Hoysalas to establish their own. However, the magnificent temples survived. People continued visiting them and believed that it was Queen Shantala's spirit that had saved these temples from total destruction.

THE PRINCESS AND THE IDOL

Alauddin Khilji of the Khilji dynasty was one of the most powerful kings in the history of the Delhi Sultanate. He ruled at the turn of the 14th century. To satisfy his bottomless greed, from time to time, he would send his army to plunder and loot the rich southern kingdoms. During one such campaign, a great amount of wealth was looted from the Srirangam Temple, located in the area known as Tamil Nadu today. The spoils included a special idol that caught the attention of Khilji's daughter. The story portrays the princess's tryst with the idol including her arrival at the Srirangam Temple in search of it. The incident of the princess's visit is mentioned in the temple's records, known as Koil Olugu. *Today, visitors to the temple can see a painting of the princess in a room considered to have been her place of worship. The temple subsequently sanctified the princess as Tulukka Nachiyar, which means 'Muslim dancer' in the local language.*

The princess was watching from her own little space in the palace of her father, Sultan Alauddin Khilji. She was not allowed to come out of the women's quarters. What she saw astonished her. There were such riches on display in her father's court!

The army general, Malik Kafur, presented himself before her father. Both his gait and countenance exhibited triumph.

'Well done, well done!' said Alauddin Khilji and embraced his general. 'I hear the region south of the Vindhya hills is now in our grasp.'

Malik Kafur nodded. He then recounted how he and his army had penetrated the unknown, hilly region and managed to attack the kingdoms of Hoysala and Kakatiya. Their opponents had put up a brave fight but soon lost. The Pandyas were very powerful, but internal strife and squabbles within the royal family weakened them, and so Malik Kafur was able to overpower them as well. He displayed the booty he had collected from ransacking these places. The sultan devoured the gold, silver, pearls, precious gems and intricately carved temple jewellery with his eyes.

The princess strained her ears to listen to what Malik Kafur was saying.

'The temples in the south are full of riches. Their deities are adorned with fabulous jewels and most of them are now part of our treasury,' Malik Kafur added proudly. The sultan's pleasure knew no bounds.

Among the riches that were on display was a small idol. It stood out among the rest of the treasure. It caught the attention of the sultan – and his daughter.

'What's this?' the sultan asked his general.

'That's a prized possession of the Srirangam Temple in Tamizhagam territory. On our journey back, we happened to pass the temple town of Srirangam. We saw this idol of Lord Ranganatha being taken around in a procession on a magnificent chariot. It was easy enough to get our hands on it. Most of the people fell prey to our attack. The remaining ones ran away. Everything in the chariot was ours to claim.'

The princess could not her take her eyes off the idol. She was completely enchanted by it and wanted it for herself.

Alauddin Khilji got busy with official matters for the rest of the day. When the princess met him at the dinner table at night, she expressed her desire to keep the idol. Her father did not think much of it. The palace jeweller had identified the metal with which it was made as *panchaloha*, a special alloy of gold, silver, copper, iron and lead. Since the treasury was overflowing with pure silver and gold and many other precious jewels, the sultan had no regrets about parting with it and let his daughter keep it. Overjoyed, she took it to her chamber.

The sultan's daily routine was to first meet his courtiers at the durbar to discuss various political issues and give appropriate orders. He would then meet his subjects and listen to their grievances and offer solutions.

The princess took a keen interest in her father's duties as a ruler. As she was not allowed in the durbar, she tried to observe the goings-on from wherever she could outside of it. She was proud of his military achievements. She had heard stories of how he had defeated the unstoppable force of the Mongols who would have otherwise reduced the land to nothing, and how he had established the Delhi Sultanate in all its glory. But she wished he would restrain his thirst for power that led to ruthless tactics, battles and bloodshed.

One day, there were some unusual visitors at the durbar. The sultan was surprised and suspicious to find a group of devout Hindus seeking permission to see him. Nevertheless, he welcomed them. They bowed respectfully and announced that they hailed from Srirangam. They brought simple presents like sandalwood, incense and long yards of pure, shimmering silk. They spoke humbly. From her perch, the princess pricked up her ears to listen to them.

'We are from the land of the Tamils. Ours is a goodwill mission. Let our flourishing land and the great Delhi Sultanate be friends for years to come.' They then chanted in unison from their holy texts and sang soulful hymns that filled the hearts of the listeners.

The sultan was touched by the simplicity and sincerity of their intentions. He clapped in appreciation. The princess too wished them well, silently.

'Well done, my friends,' said the sultan. 'Tell me, what would you like as a token of friendship?'

The leader of the group stepped forward and said with extreme regard, 'If the honourable sultan could give us the idol of Sri Ranganatha that has been brought to the sultanate…' Before he could finish, the sultan exploded with laughter.

'Is that all you want?' he asked. 'Granted,' he added in a louder voice.

The princess was aghast. *The…the idol is mine. How can he just give it away?* she thought in dismay. Unable to hold herself back, she dashed into the durbar and said, 'Father! The idol is mine. You can't give it away!'

Everyone was shocked, but the sultan remained calm. He was fond of his daughter. He replied kindly, 'I can't go back on my word, my dear child. I will get you a hundred more of such idols.'

The princess shook her head, cupped her mouth with her hand and ran away, blinking back her tears. That night, as she tossed and turned in her bed, she came up with a plan.

The next day, when the party from Srirangam was about to start its journey, the princess sneaked out of the palace and approached them. She pleaded with them to return the idol, but they refused.

'Then I will go with you to Srirangam,' she said passionately. 'The idol is mine. I will not be parted from it.'

'Please, don't! You cannot come with us. Sooner or later the sultan will come to know that you are gone, and he'll promptly chop our heads off,' they said with fear mounting in their hearts.

The stubborn princess turned a deaf ear to their pleas. While they looked on helplessly, she quickly pulled out a few of their clothes from their luggage, changed into them and began to travel with them as a part of the group.

When the princess was found missing in the palace, there was pandemonium all around. The sultan was ablaze with anger and dark with grief.

'Those wretched men from Srirangam! They have kidnapped my daughter! Do they think I'll pay them a huge ransom to get her back?' he fumed.

He called for his army general, Malik Kafur. Taking a deep, determined breath, he commanded, 'Take your army and leave immediately. Get those wretched "goodwill" men from wherever they are. Bring our princess back and get rid of them. In case they've harmed her in any way, spare one of them and get him to lead you to Srirangam through the shortest possible route. Not a single soul should be seen alive there. Not a single brick or stone of the temple should be left standing.'

Malik Kafur's head reeled. 'Go back all the way beyond the Vindhyas?' he asked himself. The army needed to rest, but he did not dare to speak. He saw how enraged the sultan was. His command would have to be obeyed at any cost. Without a word, the general bowed deeply and left to make preparations to carry out the orders. Soon, he was leading the royal army southwards.

The princess and the group were travelling as fast as they could on foot. Suddenly, the princess stopped.

'Can you feel the tremors?' she asked.

No one answered.

'Is it an earthquake,' asked one of the men.

'No. I know the sound,' continued the princess. 'Horses' hooves. My father's army is after us.' The group made a lightning-quick decision. One of them took the princess and disappeared in a different direction. Another carried the idol and followed yet another route. The rest gave themselves up to the sultan's army. Malik Kafur spared just one of them, who, under threat of death, led the army to Srirangam.

The princess and her escort reached the temple ahead of the army, but the idol and its escort were nowhere to be seen.

'Where is my idol?' cried the princess, heartbroken. 'Gone? Lost?' she sobbed. Then, through her sobs, more thoughts popped up in her mind. 'My idol is a part of the temple. It will come back here some day, and I'll live here with it. I'll dance in the temple along with the devadasis, the temple dancers. But, for now, the temple must be saved from my father's soldiers. I cannot let it be ransacked. 'Not a moment to waste. Hurry!' she told the priests. They worked all night to clear the temple as far as they could and raised a brick wall to hide the sanctum sanctorum.

By the time they were done, the entire place looked deserted. The princess and the devadasis crept through an underground passage that led them out of the temple to a safer place.

Malik Kafur and his army thundered into Srirangam. They stood and gazed in awe at the grandeur and sheer size of the temple. But that did not steer them away from their determination to plunder and rob the temple. It took them days to go around plundering, killing everyone in sight.

When the army neared the sanctum sanctorum, the general roared with laughter.

'Ha! Just a brick wall to protect the most precious part of the temple!' he exclaimed and commanded his army to break it. 'Down goes the wall and in we go to loot the temple treasures,' he yelled.

Beyond the wall, the sanctum sanctorum was difficult to break into. When, at last, they plunged into the dark chamber, they found it empty.

'Those wily scoundrels!' cried the general, his voice sinking with disappointment. 'They have relocated their treasures.' The next moment, he commanded in his thunderous voice, 'The loss of our princess has to be avenged to whatever extent possible. Do not stop pillaging. Charge ahead!' The killings and destruction continued.

After they had caused enough bloodshed and destruction, the army turned and began to march back with whatever they had looted. Malik Kafur had a last look at the broken remains of the temple.

Not long afterwards, dark clouds gathered in the sky. There were bright flashes of lightning followed by deafening thunder. Monsoon rains poured from the heavens, and Srirangam was drenched. Life came to a standstill everywhere. The heavy rains caught the returning army unawares. The soldiers had to wade through the water and slush, and many lost their lives. Imagining their plight, the princess sighed sadly.

The army was a much smaller unit when it reached the Delhi Sultanate. With a heavy heart, thc gcncral told the sultan about their failure to locate the princess's whereabouts.

'But her loss has been avenged in the most destructive way,' he added by way of consolation.

The sultan was speechless with sorrow. But deep down in his heart he knew that his daughter was safe and in the temple premises.

The princess danced along with the devadasis in the temple after it was restored, it is said, hoping that her cherished idol would be found one day. But this did not happen and the haunting memories of it soon took her life.

THE KING WHO WOULD TAKE NO DEFEAT

Vijayanagar was an extensive empire in south India from the 14th to the 16th century. It spanned a good part of modern-day Karnataka and some parts of Andhra Pradesh, Telangana and Kerala. Krishnadevaraya is hailed as the greatest king of Vijayanagar. During his reign, the kingdom flourished. At the same time, he was surrounded by powerful sultanates that were eyeing his kingdom. Battle followed battle but the enemy forces were thwarted each time – Krishnadevaraya did not lose a single fight. The king's efficient administration and care for his subjects made the kingdom prosperous. He was a great patron of the arts, and many artistically designed granite palaces, temples, pavilions and gateways were built under his patronage.

After Krishnadevaraya, Vijayanagar could not withstand the attacks of its enemies and was soon ruined. But the spirit of the empire continues to live on even today. The imposing ruins of the temples at Hampi are proof of the former glory of Vijayanagar.

'Krishna,' his mother called out, her hands dripping with gingelly oil. 'Come and sit here.' The boy came running and sat on the wooden seat in front of her. He was bare-bodied – only a loincloth was tied round his hips. His mother smeared the oil on his body. Even his face was not spared. He squeezed his eyes shut and wrinkled his nose. Unmindful of his grimace, his mother continued to massage him gently yet firmly for a while longer. Krishna stared at the scars on his hands and feet. When the massage was over, he jumped up and ran to have a bath. It was an everyday routine.

'How long will you keep doing this, Amma?' Krishna asked his mother.

'For as long as I can, dear. When you are older, you'll have a man to do it for you. You will have strong limbs then and his powerful hands will massage them well,' she replied.

'But why do I need a massage at all?'

'Well, do you see the scars on your skin?'

Krishna nodded. 'How can I not see them?'

'They are marks from a deadly disease called smallpox that you were afflicted with when you were younger. By God's grace, you recovered, but the scars remained. They are harmless now. The oil massage will make them look less prominent in course of time. The disease made your limbs weak. The massage will make them strong again, so that when you grow up, you can gallop away on your horse and learn the art of warfare.'

His mother's words brought a sparkle to young Krishna's eyes.

One day, during the morning massage ritual, Krishna asked, 'Amma, will you tell me a story?'

'Story? What kind of story do you want to hear? Of gods and demons or adventure?'

'No, Amma. Tell me about our land, Vijayanagar. It is called the Land of Victory, isn't it?'

His mother smiled. 'It is a long story, Krishna. Vijayanagar was not built in a day,' she began. 'The towering temples, the granite palaces, the artistic gateways, the massive forts and whatever else you see took many years to build. A long time ago, our ancestors acquired the fertile land along the banks of the silvery river Tungabhadra. We faced many invaders and fought as many battles. Several were won, some were lost. Riches were looted, people were killed… But we survived. We had tenacity, courage, will power and tactics.'

After finishing her narration, she said, 'Tomorrow, I'll tell you about two very special people from our clan, Harihara and Bukka Raya, whom everyone called Hakka and Bukka.'

'Hakka, Bukka! That sounds funny,' shrieked an excited Krishna.

'That may be, but we must bow to them. Vijayanagar was born in their hands. I will tell you the rest tomorrow,' she said, getting up, while Krishna went for his bath.

The next day, his mother continued from where she had left off.

'Hakka and Bukka were the sons of a local chieftain in the tiny kingdom of Kampili on the banks of the Tungabhadra. The brothers were brave fighters. When Muhammad bin Tughlaq, a powerful sultan who ruled north India, came with his army to plunder the rich kingdoms of the south, including Kampili, Hakka and Bukka fought them valiantly. But Kampili's army was no match for the sultan's soldiers. The king of Kampili was killed and the brothers were taken as prisoners of war.'

'What's so great about them if they became the sultan's prisoners?' asked Krishna.

'Patience… I'm coming to that. They impressed the sultan so much that he asked them to lead his army in its next looting expedition in the south. Hakka and Bukka had been waiting for a chance like this.

'It was past sunset when the army led by Hakka and Bukka reached the banks of the Tungabhadra. The army camped for the night. The soldiers rested, all except Hakka and Bukka. They did not waste a single moment and rushed to Kampili. They readied the army overnight and at daybreak, the Kampili army attacked the sultan's men. Caught by surprise, the sultan's soldiers were unable to retaliate. They turned and took to their heels. Hakka and Bukka won the battle!'

Krishna clapped in delight.

His mother added, 'Then, Hakka and Bukka established their own kingdom on the southern banks of Tungabhadra and called it the 'Land of Victory' or Vijayanagar.'

Krishna jumped up. 'I will not let them down! I'll make Vijayanagar even more glorious when I become king.'

'Poor boy,' his mother sighed and said to herself, 'he doesn't know that he is second in the line of succession to the throne.' Krishna's elder brother had ascended the throne and his son was being groomed to be the next king.

Krishna grew up to be a strong young man. He would be up before dawn every day and go for his horse-riding lessons. He looked forward to galloping around the countryside with the cool morning breeze brushing his face.

After riding, it was massage time for him. Over the years, he had grown to like this ritual. Glistening with oil, he would get ready for his next activity – wrestling. His opponent, equally oily, would grip him tightly and the two would wrestle till they puffed, panted and perspired. Krishna always won the game except for once when his attention was diverted by a mongoose running across the area. That day, Krishna understood the importance of undivided attention, and this lesson stood him in good stead in the wars he fought later.

Krishna showed keen interest in the art of warfare. He was adept at wielding the sword, and he soon became a skilled warrior.

A curious turn of events in history made Krishna the ruler of Vijayanagar after all. His brother, the king, on his deathbed, decided that Krishna would be the best choice to preserve the honour of the Land of Victory. He placed the crown on his brother's head before breathing his last.

Krishna was happy to be king. At the same time, he feared his enemies. Vijayanagar was surrounded by greedy, ruthless sultanates. They lost no time in attacking Vijayanagar when they learnt of the previous king's demise. However, with Krishnadevaraya at the helm, Vijayanagar's forces fearlessly faced the enemy armies and drove them back. He rewarded the good fighters and saw that the wounded were attended to.

For a while, there was peace in Vijayanagar. Krishnadevaraya could turn his attention to the welfare of the land. Krishna felt that the prestige of Vijayanagar would reach greater heights if they could recapture two of their strongest forts that had been lost by the earlier kings to their neighbours in the Kalinga region.

He expressed his thoughts to his war minister, Thimmarasu, who agreed with him.

'Then get our forces ready,' commanded the king.

Soon, the army marched towards the fort of Udayagiri. It was challenging to approach the fort, because it was situated on top of a rugged hill and the path to reach it was narrow. The army progressed slowly but resolutely. Even showers of arrows and the thunder of cannons from the enemy's side did not stop the soldiers from marching ahead. The king got the path widened and the army poured into the fort brandishing their swords. Surprised by the ambush, the enemy garrison panicked and surrendered.

The other fort, Kondaividu, was a greater challenge. The fort's walls were strong and impenetrable. Krishnadeva's army began to tire.

'This won't do. We are losing time, men and arms,' the king told his general. 'We have to change our strategy.'

He directed his men to build tall wooden platforms, which were dragged to the walls of the fort. The soldiers could now climb up these platforms, reach the top of the fort walls and vault over them.

Once Krishnadeva's men were inside, the two armies clashed in a fierce battle. The king instructed Thimmarasu to aim his special fire-tipped arrow from above at the storage space in the fort. The place burst into flames. The frightened enemy soldiers lost their nerve. The Vijayanagar forces had triumphed and claimed the fort as theirs.

The sultans were enraged by their defeat. They joined hands and planned a retaliation.

'This time, it will be a two-pronged attack. The wily Krishnadeva will not escape,' they swore.

When Krishnadeva came to know about the advancing army, he told Thimmarasu, 'Prepare our men. You will lead one half of the army and I'll take the other. We have to cover the entire area between the rivers Krishna and Tungabhadra, wherever the enemy army is spread out.'

The Vijayanagar army set out with a huge force of elephants, horses and soldiers on foot. The king also arranged for water carriers and cooks to be stationed at the base camp. Scouts were sent ahead to determine the spread of the enemy's men.

At the crack of dawn, the mood grew tense. Suddenly, the Vijayanagar army let out a fearsome war cry and sounded the battle drums; it seemed like the heavens were crashing down. In the blink of an eye, the Vijayanagar army spread itself in six different directions. Krishnadeva and Thimmarasu led the attack in the two most crucial directions. The explosion of the sultan's cannons tore the air. A few of Krishnadeva's men fell prey to the deadly cannons, but the others managed to dodge them. The Vijayanagar army forced their way right into the middle of the enemy forces. Wherever they turned, the enemy soldiers found Krishnadeva's men attacking them. Too frightened to wield their weapons, they fled to the safety of their base camp.

There was devastation in Krishnadeva's army too. The rivers proved fatal for the men and animals. But ultimately, it was a crushing defeat for the sultanate army and an awesome victory for Vijayanagar.

After defeating the sultans, Krishnadeva proceeded to capture the strategically important Raichur fortress. He cleverly took the help of the Portuguese musketeers led by one of their generals. The Vijayanagar army made a quick job of seizing the citadel and brought it under their control in no time. Krishnadeva's list of victories was now finally complete.

That autumn, when Vijayanagar celebrated its annual Mahanavami festival, it also celebrated Krishnadevaraya's victories. The palace, temples, bazaars and houses – all were lit up gloriously. Gifts were distributed generously and there was a splendid feast. There were performances by dancers, musicians, magicians and clowns for everyone's entertainment. The people enjoyed the sight of the magnificent parade of the soldiers and the caparisoned elephants and horses.

At last, peace reigned in the Land of Victory. Krishnadeva worked tirelessly for his kingdom. He saw to it that the officials did their jobs properly and the people carried on comfortably with farming and other occupations like weaving and woodcraft. Vijayanagar was not only a land of victory but a land of prosperity as well.

Krishnadevaraya promoted art and culture during those days of peace. He enjoyed watching people of talent and eminence display their skills in court. One such person was Ramakrishna who was a migrant from Tenali in Andhra Pradesh. The king was impressed by his intelligence and scholarship, and he recruited him as his special adviser. Several issues of the state were solved amicably with the help of Ramakrishna's ready wit and wisdom.

Vijayanagar's fortunes changed when Krishnadeva contracted an illness and died in his forties. The kings who came after him were not as strong, and the land steadily lost its glory in the years to come.

THE QUEEN WHO RULED THE WAVES

Rani Abbakka belonged to the Chowta dynasty that ruled over parts of Karnataka in the 16th century. At that time, the Portuguese had come to India to trade in spices. Soon, they established themselves as a powerful political force. Seeing this, Abbakka refused to continue trading with them and set about to bring them down. In a relentless round of battles, she drove the Portuguese to desperation. Eventually, treachery and heavy losses weakened her position, but she did not give up till the very end and died fighting. Abbakka's memory is honoured during the Rani Abbakka Utsava that is celebrated in her hometown of Ullal. There are also folk-style theatrical shows known as Yakshagana *that portray her life and achievements.*

Ullal was the port capital of the kingdom of Tulunadu on the south-west coast of India. The palace of the queen, Rani Abbakka, inside the Ullal Fort overlooked the Arabian Sea. She stood in the balcony adjoining her bedchamber, gazing at the glorious sunset. The sea was about to devour the ball of fire. Soon, Tulunadu would be enveloped in darkness.

Tulunadu was also known as Parashurama Kshetram. Abbakka recalled the legendary story her grandmother had told her about how the name came to be. Apparently, Parashurama, the sixth avatar of Lord Vishnu had recovered Tulunadu from the sea. When Parashurama threw his axe across the sea, the water receded as far as the axe went. The land that was thus salvaged came to be known as Tulunadu.

'A region so powerfully blessed by the Lord himself should under no circumstances be surrendered to foreigners,' she told herself with steely determination. Abbakka took a deep breath and turned round to face her mother's portrait on the eastern wall of the chamber. It glowed with the rays of the disappearing sun. Her mother had been an incredibly beautiful woman, and Abbakka looked just like her. She was glad the artist had painted the portrait before her mother's health deteriorated. The look of courage in her mother's eyes was electrifying. Now that she was no more, the portrait served as a memory of her.

On the southern wall was another picture. Abbakka's mother had personally supervised the artist while he made it. The picture was that of a Portuguese ship on fire. In the last battle that Abbakka's mother had fought with the Portuguese, she had shown her defiance by burning their ship. Yet, she lost. She had vowed to win the battle, but it did not happen. It was a big blow for her, and it affected her physically. In a short period of time, her health took a turn for the worse and she passed away. Abbakka was by her side during her last days. She took good care of her mother, and promised to do her best to protect the land and the people of Tulunadu.

The Chowta dynasty's system of inheritance was matrilineal*. Accordingly, Abbakka was crowned

* A person's lineage traced through the mother's family line

queen by her maternal uncle, Thirumala Raya. He was also the one to arrange her marriage with Veera Narasimha, the king of a principality close to Ullal.

Abbakka learnt the nuances of warfare and military strategy from her uncle, reminding herself that she needed to be as formidable as her mother.

One day, Abbakka was awaiting the return of her ship that had gone out to sea on a trading trip. The sun had risen to a scorching height, but there was no sign of the vessel. Abbakka decided to send her expert oarsmen to look for it.

'As you wish, Raniamma. We'll trace the ship in no time,' they said enthusiastically and left. They loved and respected their young and valiant queen.

It took a while for the oarsmen to return. Abbakka's heart started beating fast when she saw them return pale-faced and dejected. They reported that the Portuguese had captured her ship.

The queen was beside herself with fury. 'Those trouble-mongers!' she hissed. 'They have done enough damage during my mother's reign, but not anymore. I won't let them.' She raised her sword and commanded her generals, 'Get ready to attack! We have to get our ship back.'

Abbakka's warship sailed into the sea and began spewing fiery arrows at the enemy. It was difficult to fight on sea as both ships were bobbing up and down among the waves. Even then, Abbakka's arrows did not miss their target. As the flaming arrows hit the Portuguese ship, its sails caught fire. Burnt and charred, they crumbled and fell into the water. Parts of the ship, along with the soldiers, went up in flames, lighting up the night sky. As the sky lost its brightness, smoke shrouded the atmosphere. The soldiers left in the enemy ship, jumped into smaller boats and sailed away to safety. Abbakka got her ship back, though it was completely looted. Nevertheless, Ullal celebrated the victory of their battle on the sea.

The seashore was littered with half-burnt bodies of soldiers and the remains of the Portuguese ship; it would take days to clear the shore.

All was quiet for the next few days. The enemy seemed to have backed off. Veera Narasimha, however, warned his wife, 'This does not mean all is well. The Portuguese are most certainly preparing for a major attack…'

'So what?' Abbakka cut in. 'We will fight them again.'

'They are far too powerful. The sea is no longer a free-trade zone. One must pay tax on goods imported via the sea route. If we just pay them what they demand, we can carry on with our business as usual.'

'Ridiculous! Pay them to use our seas and bow down to them? I'll never do that.'

Narasimha lost his temper. 'You can't be so stubborn! This is a battle you cannot win!'

'What if I do?' said Abbakka.

Dejected, Narasimha shook his head. 'You're going to lose the kingdom. I can't help you anymore. Don't say I didn't warn you.'

Abbakka stood her ground and watched her husband walk away.

Later, Abbakka's daughter Abhaya asked her, 'Amma, why did you have to quarrel with Appa over this issue? What if he is right? What if the enemy cannot be defeated?'

'Abhaya, even if what he says is correct, I don't have a place either in my heart or in Ullal for cowards who have no regard for the prestige of the motherland,' Abbakka replied with a resolute shrug. Abhaya silently agreed with her mother and admired her courage of conviction.

History's fingers trembled with awe as she steadily continued to record Abbakka's fiery words and actions.

One afternoon, Abhaya wanted to visit the rock temple dedicated to Lord Shiva that was located on the seashore, a short distance away from the palace. As Abbakka was busy, Abhaya went alone.

Abbakka cautioned her daughter, 'Be careful, Abha. The Portuguese have been seen lurking around in these parts.'

'Don't worry, Amma. I'll be careful,' Abhaya promised her mother.

Dressed in a delicate, pale-pink cotton sari, woven in the typical Ullal style, Abhaya climbed up to the temple barefoot. The sun was setting by the time she reached the temple. Suddenly, a pair of strong hands grabbed her by the shoulder. There was a tussle, and the basket of flowers and fruits she held toppled and fell. Before she could cry out, she was gagged and dragged to a dark corner of the temple.

Then, suddenly, some others appeared on the scene. They freed Abhaya and took her back to the safety of the palace. The poor girl broke down as she reported the incident to her mother.

'I suspected mischief, so I sent my men to watch over you,' said Abbakka. She was confident that her soldiers would not let any harm come to her daughter. But Abhaya was shaken by the incident and could not stop crying.

'My child,' said Abbakka gently. 'You are Abhaya, the fearless. Never forget what your name means,' she consoled her. But when Abbakka learnt that the man who had tried to kidnap her daughter had been sent by Narasimha, she was overcome with agony and rage. She stood in front of her mother's portrait and shed a bitter tear.

'Bless me, Mother, to stand alone and fight the enemy for your sake and for the sake of our people. From now on, I'll have nothing to do with my husband as he has his own vicious plans and justifies the brutality of the foreigner.'

She wiped her tears and said decisively, 'I'll fight a lone battle if I must and achieve my purpose. At least I have Abha with me.'

Many a battle was fought on sea and land. Abbakka was not one to give up easily, and she fought relentlessly.

The Portuguese were amazed at her strategies. Never had they lost so many men and ships in battle. They decided to change tactics and aimed their cannons at the Ullal fort. They had already plundered the major city of present-day Mangalore and built a stronghold there. They would send their fleet of cavalry and infantry well equipped with weapons from Mangalore to Ullal.

There was a thundcrous noise the day the Portuguese army began their march towards Ullal.

'For our motherland!' cried Abbakka, standing in front of her army. 'We'll fight the enemy on land or sea, on the streets or on the shore. But push them back we will!'

With a loud war cry, her soldiers advanced bravely and put up a defensive attack. But they were outnumbered by the Portuguese battalion. Cannons blasted and the enemy inched into Ullal steadily. After some time, they triumphantly entered the royal premises. But, to their utter dismay, they found it deserted. Suddenly, there was nothing for them to do; no sword wielding, no gun shooting, no cannon blasting. So, they sent word to Mangalore and waited for instructions.

Abbakka, however, hadn't abandoned her home. She had simply slipped away from the fort and taken refuge in an abandoned mosque where no one would come looking for her. She had a few of her brave soldiers with her, alert and waiting. In the fading twilight, she marched into Ullal with her men.

The sight of the queen's army unnerved the enemy soldiers who had let their guard down while awaiting further orders. They had no weapons at the ready, and Abbakka's soldiers could defeat them easily.

The Portuguese were beside themselves with rage and desperation. They swore to give a final savage blow to the pesky queen of Ullal and sound her death knell. Once again, they prepared to face her. This time, they got Abbakka's husband Narasimha to reveal her war strategies to them for a fee. It helped them greatly to prepare for a final battle with the Queen of the Seas.

Abbakka did not wait for them to attack. She marched bravely to Mangalore and entered the Portuguese stronghold. However, with Narasimha on their side, the Portuguese were prepared this time. The battle inside the fort did not last long. Abbakka's strategies were not a surprise anymore and so they had no power over the enemy.

Abbakka died in captivity. Her final thoughts were about her mother and her daughter. She said to herself, 'Mother, I did my best to protect our land. Now Abhaya will take over and uphold our legacy.' And sure enough, Abhaya, began to rule Tulunadu with courage and conviction. She came to be known as Abbakka the Third. True to her lineage, she reigned for a few years, bravely fighting battles to the last. Eventually, the Portuguese overpowered a large part of the coastal region, including Tulunadu.

History has recorded very little of Abbakka's life and reign. Much more has been said about the might of the Portuguese and things they did to establish themselves as a power to be reckoned with.

THE TRIBAL QUEEN

Gondwana, a tribal region in the northern Deccan plateau was ruled by Rani Durgavati – an indomitable warrior – in the 16th century. She was a Rajput princess who married a Gond prince. The throne of Gondwana unexpectedly fell vacant for her. She fought the sultans in many a battle but died in a final battle against the Mughal army. There is an illustration of this battle in Akbar's biography that depicts Durgavati being struck by the fatal arrow. A copy of it is currently in the London Museum. Poets have written verses praising her valour, and Gond tribals sing about her bravery even today. This story is based on her life and depicts scenes of her reign and the final battle that she fought riding on her favourite war elephant.

Durgavati was up before dawn, ready to go riding on her golden mare. Gathering speed, the two of them were soon galloping through the thick forests of the Satpura hills. Durgavati threw back her head and took a deep breath, drinking in the coolness of the grey dawn. Silhouetted against the brightening sky, she was the picture of joyful confidence. Her father – the Chandela Rajput ruler of Mahoba – had taught her to ride horses and wield weapons even before she became a teenager.

Her mare slowed down when she heard the familiar hoof beats of a stallion coming from the opposite direction. The two horses met, and so did the riders. The stallion bore on his back the stately figure of Dalpat Shah, the eldest son of the Gond tribal chief, Sangram Shah.

'How are you this morning, my lovely?' asked Dalpat Shah.

'As good as you my…not-so-lovely…ha! ha!' Durgavati teased.

They rode together, racing each other for a while.

'Let me go back before my father decides to send his troops to look for me,' said Durgavati after some time. Then, the two riders went their separate ways, back to their respective homes.

Mornings in the Rajput palace were always busy, but that day, it was busier than usual. It was the auspicious day of Durgashtami. Preparations were going on for the special prayer to be held at the palace shrine in honour of Goddess Durgadevi. It was also Durgavati's birthday, her eighteenth one. She prayed fervently to the Goddess, asking her to shape her future well.

Once the puja was over, Durgavati knew that her father would bring up the topic of her marriage, and she was ready with her answer.

'Durga, my child,' said her father. 'You have turned eighteen today. You are old enough for marriage now. I have in mind a brave, young Rajput prince who would be a suitable life partner for you.'

After a moment's pause, Durgavati said firmly, 'Father, I will marry Dalpat Shah, the crown prince of Gondwana, and no one else.'

The silence that followed was uncomfortable. Durgavati's father's face turned dark with annoyance.

'You're asking for the impossible, Durga. A Rajput princess marrying a tribal prince… Ridiculous! No, never!' he said, pacing around the room with his hands clasped behind his back. But Durgavati stayed firm.

The next morning, as usual, dawn watched the two horse riders meet. Durgavati told Dalpat what had happened between her and her father and added, 'Take me to your home right now if you care for me. I'm not going back to my father's palace to be married off to a Rajput prince, no matter how handsome he may be.' The two riders wasted no

time. They turned direction and rode like the wind to Gondwana.

Sangram Shah was glad to welcome Durgavati, but he was also a man of principles. So, he asked Durgavati to go back home, promising that he would come later to formally ask her father for her hand in marriage to his son. Durgavati could not refuse. She went back home and waited.

Sangram Shah arrived in a royal procession and a fanfare of trumpets. He brought many gifts for Durgavati and her family, but her father was not impressed. He did not want his daughter living as a princess in a tribal kingdom, no matter how powerful or rich it was. However, seeing the princess's resolve, he had no choice but to bend to her will.

Garlands were exchanged and wedding bells pealed in both the kingdoms. There was boundless rejoicing everywhere. Among several other things, Durgavati's father gave her a special gift – a stately war elephant.

'This is for you, my dear Durga – so daring in love. And so you shall be in war too.'

Durgavati was thrilled! Proudly, she showed off the gift to Dalpat. She decided to make the elephant her personal mount and named him Smaran, meaning remembrance. She and Dalpat travelled through the forests, as they had before their marriage. Durgavati sat on Smaran while Dalpat rode his favourite horse. Sometimes, the couple wielded swords and sparred together. Dalpat admired Durgavati's warrior-like spirit.

The ring of the wedding bells had barely subsided when the alarming boom of war drums began to sound in the Chandela kingdom. Tension soared as Sher Shah Suri, the mighty Afghan general, and his army marched towards Durgavati's homeland.

The Chandela king was unprepared. His army was insignificant compared to the sultan's massive one. The enemy's infantry and cavalry tore through the region. Chandela had to take the help of Gondwana.

Sangram Shah readily lent his forces and Durga let Smaran go to war too.

Cannons exploded all around along with gun shots. Thousands of glistening swords clashed in the air. It was a fierce battle that lasted for days. The sky turned red, reflecting the blood that flowed in the battlefield. Countless lives were lost. At long last, Chandela arrows pierced Sher Shah Suri's armour fatally. His army lost its morale and withdrew, and the devastating battle ended. Durgavati's father was now glad he had made a marriage alliance with the Gonds. Without the support of Sangram Shah's army, he could not have survived the war.

A few days after the din of war had subsided, another significant event took place, and this time, it was at Gondwana. Vir Narayan was born to Durgavati and Dalpat Shah.

Vir was only six months old when Durgavati took him on his first elephant ride. Smaran's war wounds had healed by then. Vir gurgled with pleasure. He patted Smaran and lisped 'Sarman' as he tried saying the animal's name.

'So, you want to call him Sarman, huh?' said Durgavati laughing. 'Well, so be it.' The elephant nodded and trumpeted in agreement.

The time came for Dalpat to be crowned king. The ceremony was a grand event. Offerings were made to the tribal gods. Food and gifts were distributed in plenty to the people. Music and merriment filled the air.

Under the leadership of King Dalpat Shah and Queen Durgavati, the kingdom was peaceful and prosperous. The damages of war were made good and Vir Narayan grew up happily. But when Vir was just five years old, Dalpat suddenly took ill and passed away. Durgavati was shattered. She decided to follow the Rajput tradition and end her life as well in his funeral pyre.*

Tongues of flame shot up from the pyre in the backyard of the palace. Dressed in white, Durgavati stood in front of it with folded hands. The heat scorched her skin, but she did not flinch. The world and its people were lost to her. In a trance, she began to advance towards the pyre. Her steps were heavy but deliberate.

The flames were about to engulf her when, suddenly, a shrill cry rang out, 'Ma! Where are you?'

Durgavati froze. The cry hammered at her senses. She was jolted back into the world when she recognized whose cry it was. She turned and rushed to the palace.

* Practising this custom is illegal as per the Indian Constitution.

Running up to Vir, Durgavati gathered her son in her arms and wept.

'Oh, Vir...I shall not leave you and go,' she whispered in his ears. Her warm tears wet his back and he wriggled out of her arms.

In that moment, Durgavati underwent a transformation. She turned to the people of Gondwana and addressed them.

'Vir Narayan is your new king, and I shall rule as the queen-regent till he is old enough to shoulder the responsibilities of the kingdom.'

The pall of gloom that had descended on the people lifted like magic. They shouted in joy, 'Long live King Vir Narayan! Hail to Rani Durgavati!'

Durgavati proved to be an able queen. The kingdom flourished under her competent guidance. with things going well in the region, Durgavati turned her attention to her neighbours. She realized that her state was flanked by the kingdoms of powerful sultans. Her mind was flooded with worrisome thoughts.

'A minor king with a queen-regent...easy to defeat... That's what they must all be thinking, twirling their moustaches,' she said to Dalpat in her heart.

'There's your brother at home, ready to grab power from my hands, and then there are the sultans, getting ready for war. I will have to face them... I will fight them all. I will not give up... And I know you will be with me in spirit,' She shed a silent tear in Dalpat's memory, her pillar of support.

The battles happened in quick succession. Arrows whizzed by and swords clanged; cannons boomed, and shots were fired; horses neighed and human voices yelled in pain. Blood flowed in rivulets. Durgavati was at her fiercest on the battlefield. Each time, she routed the enemies so thoroughly that the enemy soldiers fled for their lives.

Now, only the brutal attack of the great Mughal emperor Akbar remained. It was well known that his army was invincible, but Durgavati was ready to face it. Undaunted, she positioned her army at strategic points across the narrow gorges to launch a surprise attack.

When Akbar's army advanced, Durgavati's army general rode ahead. She herself was on Samran while Vir Narayan rode his sturdy steed.

'It is going to be difficult, Vir,' Durgavati called out, raising her voice above the din of the battlefield as the two armies approached each other.

'Remember, death before dishonour,' were her parting words to him as he galloped ahead.

The exploding cannons created havoc. Soon, the battle became bloody. Soldiers fought and soldiers fell. Wounded horses ran helter-skelter. Elephants stampeded as they rushed ahead.

Durgavati shot arrows with amazing precision, felling men by the hundreds. Arrows that whizzed past her missed her by a hair's breadth. But Vir was not so lucky. Hit by a sword-wielding soldier on horseback, Vir fell from his steed and was gravely injured. He was rushed back to the camp to be treated,

No one waited for the sun to rise. At the crack of dawn, the battle drums were pounded. The animals let out their war cry. Soldiers fastened their armour and gathered their weapons. The earth quaked as the armies marched towards each other.

It was the fiercest battle ever. Durgavati's general noticed with a pang of fear that the Mughal army far outnumbered their own. It did not take long for their numbers to dwindle further. Durgavati could no longer be protected from the torrent of enemy arrows. Soon enough, one of them pierced her right temple and another struck her neck.

She knew her end was near.

Instantly, she drew her sword and stabbed herself to death. Sarman felt her slump heavily on his back. Without waiting a moment longer in the battlefield, he turned around and sped back to the camp.

Although he had won her kingdom, Akbar felt he had lost the battle. He had failed to take Durgavati alive as his prisoner.

Vir Narayan, who had managed to survive, gave his mother a funeral befitting a queen and a warrior. He was proud of her.

'The world will remember her for her grit and firmness of purpose,' he told himself. The people of Gondwana prayed for their brave queen who fought unyieldingly till her death on the battlefield.

KINGS AND ANIMALS

Emperor Akbar's biography, Akbar Nama, *by Abul Fazal, records the emperor's extraordinary love for animals like camels, elephants and cheetahs. European explorers and other visitors to the Mughal court have also recorded it. Akbar's son, Jahangir, was fascinated by animals as well. His meticulously maintained journals have proved to historians that he was a true naturalist with an insatiable curiosity about animals. The British and French in India during the 16th century were astonished by his attraction to unusual pets like the zebra and the stag. This story is based on the relationship that these two great Mughals had with their pets.*

Emperor Jahangir had had a busy morning at the royal court. There were guests from far and near who had come to discuss important matters with him. After a sumptuous lunch, the emperor retired to his palace for a siesta. In the evening, when he walked into the palace garden for a stroll, he saw an unusual sight. There was a strange-looking animal standing under the lemon tree.

Who brought this creature here? he wondered. There was no one in sight. Being fond of animals, he could not resist the urge to take a closer look at the quadruped. His children had accompanied him on the stroll and weren't far behind. They ran up to their father.

'Keep away!' Jahangir called out sternly. The children stepped back quickly and continued watching from a distance. They saw their father looking keenly at the creature in front of him. He held its mouth in the palm of his left hand. Then, with his right hand he gently opened its jaw and started counting its teeth. The creature snorted and twitched its ears. Jahangir patted its back and went round it as he tapped its sides and underside. Going over to the animal's hindquarters, he lifted and felt its short, black, tufted tail.

'Hmm...is this a horse or a donkey? Doesn't seem to neigh or bray...' he muttered frowning. He continued to stare at it for a while and then ran his hands over the black stripes on its skin. He rubbed the stripes and scratched them. The animal moved a few steps ahead with a sharp, short bark.

The children could not contain themselves any longer and came rushing to their father's side.

'Abba, are you trying to scrub off the stripes? Please let us help you!' they cried.

One of them brought a bucket of water, another a mug and a third got a camel-hair brush. They took turns to scrub the stripes on the animal's back. The stripes did not fade or disappear. Instead, they became brighter than before. The children gave up.

'The stripes belong to the animal. They can't be rubbed off,' concluded one.

'It's a striped donkey,' said another.

'You know what? We should name it Stripey!' said one of them. Thrilled, the children clapped their hands and laughed while their father stood deep in thought.

Just then, they heard a voice behind them say, 'The stripes are characteristic of the animal.'

Everyone turned around to see who had spoken up. It was Mir Jafar, a capable and respectful courtier in the emperor's court.

Mir Jafar bowed deeply to Jehangir and said, 'Jahanpanah, this animal is native to the country of Ethiopia. The Turks who have come to visit us have brought it as a gift for you.'

'What do they call it?' asked Jehangir, furrowing his brow.

'They call it zebra, Jahanpanah.'

'Zebra, zebra, zebra,' the children chanted in a sing-song manner, going in circles round the animal.

Jahangir's brow cleared and his face relaxed. Pleased with the gift, he sent a note of thanks to the Turks and summoned the royal artist.

'Paint a true-to-life picture of this zebra. It shall adorn the durbar wall.'

The artist set to work, and Jahangir watched his progress with interest.

The children ran in to their mother, Nurjahan, to tell her all about the curious-looking animal. The empress listened to them with great amusement. When they were done, she said, 'A zebra in our home! How exciting! I have read about these creatures but

have never seen one so far. No two zebras in the world have the same pattern of stripes, they say.'

'How interesting!' the children exclaimed.

'Ammi,' said Salima, the oldest of them. 'What is a naturalist? I have heard Jafar Baba say that Abba is a great naturalist.'

Nurjahan laughed. She loved the company of her children but rarely got a chance to spend time with them. Helping Jahangir with the administration of the empire kept her very busy.

'Salima, I'll answer your question by and by,' she said laughing. 'But first, I'll take you all to the Hiran minaret tomorrow.'

They left early next morning. It was a long way to the minaret, but the children were too excited to mind the travel time.

The sight of the minaret made the children gasp. It stood in a vast expanse of land on top of an octagonal base and was surrounded by a square waterbody.

'The surrounding area is a hunting ground,' said Nurjahan. 'You know, your abba never went on a hunting trip without his antelope to help him. But one day, the antelope's antlers got entangled in some thorny bushes. In the blink of an eye, before Abba could have him rescued, a hungry lion pounced upon the antelope. Abba was so heartbroken. He built this minaret in that antelope's memory.'

Nurjahan continued, 'Abba's fondness for the animal kingdom and his keen interest in studying and learning about their lives is what makes him an expert naturalist, Salima.'

'But...' interrupted Khurram, '...what about his hunting expeditions? He shoots animals, doesn't he?'

Nurjahan was at a loss for a convincing answer. She was a keen huntress herself and often accompanied Jahangir on his hunting trips riding on an elephant. She realized that the two qualities – being a naturalist and a hunter – were contradictory and explained, 'The Mughal clan has always been fond of hunting. They believe that if wild animals are not killed, they will breed into dangerously large numbers and be a hazard to society.'*

Two days later, the children wanted to go for a swim. They eagerly ran to the large pool in the palace gardens, but it was cordoned off. They were told that the elephants were coming there for a swim, so it was out of bounds for everyone else.

'What? Elephants in the pool?' screamed Khusrau.

Nurjahan laughed aloud. 'That's your abba! Sometimes when his elephants find the river water

* This practice is illegal now and wild animals are protected under the law.

uncomfortably cold, he arranges for the pool water to be warmed up and enjoys watching the elephants play in it happily.'

'Ammi, has Abba inherited his passion for animals from our grandfather?' Khurram wanted to know.

'You know...I've often had the same thought,' Nurjahan confessed. 'It may be a good idea to ask your grandfather about it.' The children jumped in delight.

Seeing them all excited, Nurjahan cautioned, 'But remember, he is not in good health these days. So, we must find out if he is ready to receive us.'

'We'll pray for him,' said Salima solemnly.

The following day after lunch, Akbar summoned his grandchildren. They eagerly went to meet him, carrying a basket of ruby red pomegranates for him. Akbar loved his grandchildren. He propped himself up in his cushioned diwan and gave them a broad welcoming smile.

'Dadu! Dadu! how are you?' said the children as they settled down around him on the carpet.

'I am well enough to talk to you, little ones. Tell me, what brings you here today?' asked Akbar.

Without a moment's pause, the children asked, 'Do you like animals?'

Akbar nodded, looking pleased with the question. He sat up and began to reminisce.

'I spent my childhood with my extended family of aunts and uncles in Kabul while my parents were here in India.

'What fun my cousins and I had running around the countryside, chasing animals! The camel was the first animal that I was really fascinated by. Once, my cousin Mirza and I got hold of a camel each. We led the lumbering creatures around with a rope. In fact, we even made them race each other!' Akbar's shoulders shook with silent laughter, thinking of his Kabul days. The children giggled.

'After the race, we gave them thick, thorny, juicy leaves and plants to eat,' continued Akbar. 'I loved my camel's thick double eyelashes, his dreamy eyes and the heavy hump on his back.'

'I think the camel is the ugliest animal on earth,' remarked Khusrau.

'Hey, don't say that again!' Akbar replied in mock anger, patting Khusrau's cheek.

Akbar began to cough. He had to stop talking for a while and take a pinch of his cough powder. Nurjahan stepped out into the antechamber and was back soon with a tall silver glass, half filled with pomegranate juice that was spiced with black salt and pepper. The children too got their share of the juice along with a special snack she had prepared with dates, nuts and other dried fruit.

'Where is my share?' Akbar wanted to know.

Nurjahan smiled and said, 'It is in the kitchen, kept away for tomorrow. You may find it difficult to digest it at this late afternoon hour.'

Akbar nodded and turned back to the children.

'I refused to leave my camel in Kabul and go to Hindustan with my parents. But then they promised to get me a sturdier Indian camel that roamed the Thar desert. It was a tempting offer. So, I parted with my Kabul camel and came to Hindustan at the age of twelve.

'Soon, I forgot about my Kabul camel, because here I found another animal that I fell in love with – the elephant! There were so many of them in Hindustan. I chose the wildest of them and the mahout taught me how to tame it. Oh, the thrill of mounting the elephant on my own without the mahout's help... indescribable! Those unforgettable elephant rides... Did you know that not only can they saunter slowly but also run fast? And... Oh! Did I forget to mention Balsundar, my baby elephant? He was such a beauty. Then there was Chanchal, the naughtiest and most stubborn creature I had ever seen! He loved wine, and I made the mahout feed him fine Portuguese wine. He enjoyed it greatly.'

The children burst into peals of laughter. Akbar was thrilled to see them enjoying his stories. He asked the children, 'Now, can any of you guess which animal I named Samand Manik?'

The children looked at each other with puzzled expressions.

'"Samand Manik" means "like a ruby",' explained Akbar.

'Was it a stag?' Salima asked hesitantly.

'Far from it. Samand Manik was my favourite cheetah!' Akbar said. 'I had several cheetahs, all captured in the wilderness. I made sure no harm came to them when they were trapped.'

'Cheetahs can run very fast,' Khurram said.

'Yes, they can, Khurram. But…I have managed to outrun one. It was a long time ago…when I was a teenager.'

The children gasped collectively. The sun had set by then, and the sky was slowly turning grey. A flight of pigeons on its way to roost dotted the dull sky. Akbar gazed out of the window and something about the scene triggered another memory.

'You know, in Kabul, when all of us cousins were made to sit with a tutor, I was the one least interested in studies. Instead, what drew me to the tutor was his skill in pigeon flying. He taught me how to do it, and together we used to spend hours flying pigeons. In Hindustan, I had my own band of pigeons. They were expert sky dancers. I trained them to tumble and dip in synchrony. What an aerial spectacle it used to be! They understood my whistle signals and did my bidding…' Akbar lapsed into silence, staring at the sky as the last pigeon disappeared from sight. He closed his eyes, and his attendant gently laid him in his bed.

'Time to leave,' Nurjahan whispered to the children.

'Daduji, salaam,' the children said softly and got ready to leave.

Akbar opened his eyes and smiled. 'Khuda Hafiz. Promise me that you will always be kind to animals and birds, my dear ones. Learn to enjoy their company. Even insects are interesting to observe. I liked watching spiders spinning their webs and catching mosquitoes and flies in them…' his voice trailed off again.

The children nodded and said softly, 'We promise, Daduji.'

History does not record any Mughal after Jahangir to have been particularly interested in animals. His descendants had their own varied interests. Khurram, for instance, who was later known as Shah Jahan, had a passion for architecture and constructed several lovely buildings during his reign.

That afternoon, Akbar was happy that he had been able to pass on the stories about his unique bond with animals to his grandchildren. However, he did not live long enough to see whether the children kept their promise.

THE KING WHO DID NOT REIGN

Dara Shikoh was the eldest son of the Mughal emperor Shahjahan, but he was not destined be king. And this is precisely what makes his life story interesting. History glorifies him as a true son of India. At a time when the country was witnessing religious conflicts, he brought new hope to its people. He dedicated his life to enable people to know the true spirit of their religions.

Although Dara Shikoh was buried in an unidentified grave near Humayun's tomb, he continues to live in the hearts of people even today. Plays, books and TV serials about him that are alive well into the 21st century are a proof of this. This story is based on the memorable life of Dara Shikoh.

The silken curtains fluttered lightly in the breeze. The richness of the tapestry and the carpet looked dull in comparison to the twilight sky. Its canopy of dark-orange and pink with streaks of coral lent its brilliance to the chandelier. But all this beauty did not attract Emperor Shahjahan who was reclining on his cushioned diwan by the window. He was watching his children play in the garden. Jahanara was talking to her younger brother Dara Shikoh. Roshanara, younger than both, was simply watching the colours of the sky. Muhi-ud-Din, who later came to be known as Aurangzeb, Murad and Shah Shuja were sweating it out by wrestling with one another.

Soon, the sky lost its brilliance. It was getting too dark for the children to stay outside.

'Come inside, children,' Shahjahan called out to them.

Jahanara and Dara ran in first, followed by Roshanara. They rushed straight to their father's chamber.

'Abbajaan, are Allah and Prabhu the same person? Dara says so,' Jahanara said.

'I should think so,' replied their father. 'Everyone may not agree, but I think Dara is right.'

Dara was not paying attention to his sister or father. His eyes were on Muhi-ud-Din, who had caught a little bird in his hands.

'Let it go!' Dara shouted. 'The poor thing is flying back home for the night.'

Muhi-ud-Din frowned and looked daggers at Dara. Finally, he set the bird free. He came in with the other two boys and asked his father, 'Now what? Could you not have let us play outside a little longer?'

'It's time for namaz,' Shahjahan replied softly. 'Run to your mother and prepare for the prayers.'

Within minutes, he heard the children and Mumtaz recite the Quranic verses. He too knelt on his prayer mat and prayed silently.

Mumtaz gave the children their evening meal and then went to her husband's chamber.

The sky was now an inky blue, and the stars twinkled brightly. It was early for moonrise. Shahjahan closed his eyes lightly for a few thoughtful moments. He opened them when he heard the swish of silken garments and caught the fragrance of Mumtaz's attar. He took hold of her heavily ringed fingers and made her sit beside him.

'How are you, *azizam?*' she asked.

'As good as you are,' Shahjahan replied.

'Dara is so different from our other sons, you know,' Mumtaz began.

'In what way, *jaan*?'

'Well, he does not say his prayers mechanically. He wants to know the meaning of the verses he is reciting. He looks peaceful while praying whereas the other boys fuss and fidget. Once prayers are over, he remains lost in thought for a few moments while the others run away immediately.'

'I too have noticed that. Allah showers his blessings on him. He, the future king of the Mughal Empire, is going to be an unparalleled emperor.' Shahjahan's voice rang with pride. Mumtaz clasped his hands in hers. The two of them remained lost in thought till the clock chimed the midnight hour.

In the days to come, Shahjahan got busy with his military expeditions. He stayed away from the palace for days on end. The days turned into years, and by the time he was back home, the children were in their mid and early teens.

One morning, he tiptoed up to the study hall and watched them while they learnt their lessons. He smiled with satisfaction to see the children respectfully seated in front of the teacher, engrossed in their studies.

Mumtaz told him, 'They are learning Persian, history and military science.'

'Good. Anything else?'

'No. The children are only too ready to finish with study time and run out except for Dara. He always wants to learn more.'

'More of what?'

'He says he wants to learn Sanskrit.'

'Hmm...that's unusual. Sanskrit is a difficult language to master. But then, it depends on how keen he is, I suppose. Let me see what I can do,' remarked Shahjahan thoughtfully.

The following day, he summoned Dara to his chamber.

'Abbajaan, salaam,' Dara greeted his father warmly.

'Dara, my son, get ready to come to the durbar with me this morning,' Shahjahan said. Dara wondered why, but he did not ask any questions. Mumtaz ensured that he was dressed appropriately. She kissed him lightly on the forehead and sent him off.

At the durbar, Shahjahan introduced Dara to his council of ministers.

'Ministers, I want you all to meet Dara Shikoh – "the star brilliant" – my eldest son and heir apparent to the Mughal throne.'

All eyes were on Dara now. The prince looked confused as everyone bowed reverentially. However, he managed to compose himself, turned and bowed to his father and then to the council. Standing next to his father, Dara studied all the faces in the assembly. Suddenly, his eyes fell on a person who looked distinct from the rest. He was dressed differently and was bald – he wore no turban. Dara instantly felt pulled to him. A silent, electrifying communication took place between the two pairs of eyes.

Dara waited impatiently for the durbar session to be over. When he was alone with his father, he asked in an excited voice, 'Baba, I noticed a person in the durbar. He looked very scholarly. Who is he?'

Shahjahan smiled and replied, 'He is a learned Hindu pundit from the holy city of Varanasi, Dara. His name is Kavindracharya. He is held in high esteem by Sanskrit scholars.'

Dara jumped with joy. 'Can I learn Sanskrit from him?' he asked his father eagerly.

Shahjahan took a few seconds to think and replied, 'He is a busy person. But perhaps I could ask him to arrange for a tutor for you.'

Shahjahan met Kavindracharya with his request. The acharya nodded with a smile and said, 'I would be happy to help.'

Soon, a Sanskrit tutor was appointed to teach Dara. From then on, Dara spent more hours in the study hall. After he had finished studying the usual subjects with his brothers and sisters, he stayed on to learn Sanskrit. He stayed up until the clock struck twelve and diligently revised whatever he had learnt in class during the day.

Soon, Kavindracharya reported to the king, 'Your son is a marvel! He has mastered the language already.

He now wants to read the scriptures and delve into their depths, and...'

'...And what?' Shahjahan interrupted. He was pleased with his son's progress, but he was also concerned about the responsibilities Dara would have to shoulder when he was crowned king. Shahjahan knew that Dara would not be able to pursue his studies so passionately then.

'...And he has expressed his wish to translate the scriptures into Persian,' added the acharya.

A shade of doubt clouded the king's countenance.

'That would not be easy for Dara,' he said. 'He is the future king, as you know.'

'He is capable of handling both,' said the acharya confidently. The king, however, had his doubts.

Shahjahan's declining health led him to crown Dara as the king sooner than he expected. After a simple ceremony, Dara Shikoh sat on the golden throne as emperor of the mighty Mughal empire. Muhi-ud-Din was furious to see the crown on Dara's head.

'Abbajaan has made a terrible mistake!' he raged before his other brothers. 'Our kingdom will crumble in Dara's hands. He is fit only to be a Sanskrit pundit, not a king.'

'Don't be so harsh. Let us wait and see how he does,' Shah Shuja said, and Murad agreed.

True to his nature, Dara spent more hours with his Sanskrit books than at the durbar with the council of ministers. He let his ministers manage the affairs of the state. Muhi-ud-Din, now known as Aurangzeb, could not stand the situation anymore.

'We are with you,' said his brothers. 'Let us threaten Dara with dethronement.'

'Threaten? No, nothing short of war,' said Aurangzeb angrily.

Dara Shikoh and Aurangzeb were locked in a bitter and prolonged battle. Shahjahan's heart ached as he kept track of their struggles from the confines of his sickroom. But Aurangzeb was not one to pay heed to his father's sentiments. Jahanara tried to convince

Aurangzeb to leave Dara alone. Her words too fell on deaf ears.

Dara's passion, however, remained unchanged. He continued with his scholarly and spiritual pursuits. He met with Sufi saints, Sikh gurus and Hindu pundits to establish a relationship between his own religion and the others. His Persian translations of Sanskrit texts travelled the world over and were translated into French and German later.

Meanwhile, Aurangzeb continued with his efforts to dethrone Dara.

'The time has come to get Dara out of our way. Don't you see he is ruining everything we Mughals stand for?' he told his brothers with increasing anger.

Murad and Shah Shuja gasped. Then, Murad said feebly, 'The people like Dara. We have to be prepared for an uprising if we harm our brother.'

'I'm sure we can handle that,' said Aurangzeb boldly. 'Dara is not fit to be a Mughal emperor.'

Aurangzeb's persistent efforts bore fruit, and Dara was dethroned. The ailing Shahjahan died, and Aurangzeb crowned himself king.

Addressing the people Aurangzeb said, 'You must understand that Dara Shikoh cannot be the emperor. He does not know how to protect the empire or uphold its name.'

The people were too scared to raise their voice. In bitter silence, they watched helplessly as Dara was dressed in rags and paraded around on a chained elephant. Strangely, however, one look at Dara Shikoh's face and their bitterness dissolved. He looked serene and peaceful despite everything.

Someone remarked, 'It is the depth of his spiritual knowledge and his conviction in the oneness of all that helps him not to nurture hatred or enmity.' There were nods from the others.

Even when Aurangzeb forced the last breath out of him, Dara Shikoh remained tranquil. He nurtured no resentment or regret. The world was amazed.

THE KING OF FORTS

Chhatrapati Shivaji Maharaj, the founder of the Maratha Empire, is an all-too-well-known figure in India's history. The passion he had for capturing forts and the methods he adopted to do so were amazing. In the process, he struck fear into the formidable sultans who held sway over a large part of the subcontinent. This story is based on his adventures related to the capture of some of the strongest and most strategically located forts using guerrilla warfare tactics. His knowledge of the geography of the land, his innovative and creative expertise in warfare, and his capability to overcome challenges were remarkable.

History has recorded all this and much more in detail. Though time has taken its toll of these forts, some of them still stand as tourist attractions.

SHIVNERI FORT

Rajmata Jijabai climbed the steps slowly. Breathing heavily, she was going from her chambers to the shrine of Goddess Shivai inside the Shivneri Fort. There, she prayed for a son as valorous as Shri Ram or a daughter as fearless as Devi Durga.

On the following day, Jijabai delivered a bright, bonny baby boy. She was overjoyed, but could not share her happiness with her husband, Shahji Maharaj. He was away at Bijapur fighting battles for the sultan while she had stayed back at the fort.

Jijabai brought her son up with a lot of love and care. She named him Shivaji, after the goddess who had blessed her. She admired his bright eyes, sharp nose and pointed chin. When Shahji came to see the child, he held him fondly and threw him up in the air. Shivaji screamed in delight as his father caught him mid-air. Shahji whispered to him, 'My dear son, may you be bestowed with the courage and ability to fight many a victorious battle.'

Shivaji saw very little of his father during his growing years. Jijabai played the role of both mother and father for him. She often told young Shivaji stories from the epics and folklore of the country to instil values of piety, patriotism, generosity, bravery and a sense of duty in him.

'Even if you must face death in the line of duty, do so fearlessly,' she told him.

'What is my duty, Aai?' Shivaji wanted to know.

'As a king, it would be to fight for the people of your land and protect them,' she replied.

Shivaji's inquisitive mind asked her another question. 'But Baba is fighting for the sultan, who does not belong to our land. Is he doing his duty, then?'

Jijabai answered him patiently. 'Yes and no. Yes, because the sultan has made himself king of the land and he looks after us. No, because he sometimes turns greedy and haughty and makes people suffer.' She paused a little. Shivaji watched her silently.

She continued, 'Sooner or later, we have to take charge of our land and look after our people…the sooner, the better.'

Shivaji nodded. Jijabai wanted the idea of *swarajya* or self-rule to take root in the young boy's mind.

Shahji appointed Dadaji Kondadev to train Shivaji in the craft of kingship, and Jijabai supervised his training. He was a keen student. Within a short period of time, he became an expert shooter, rode on horseback like the wind and wielded the sword like an experienced warrior.

One morning, young Shivaji did not turn up for his lessons. Worried, Dadaji went looking for the prince. He was neither with his mother nor at his favourite spot near the water springs. Then, as Dadaji was walking past the temple, he heard Shivaji's voice. He was praying aloud at the altar.

'Oh, Shivai Ma! Bless me so that I can live up to my mother's dream to rule my land and protect my people.'

Dadaji embraced him and said, 'You surely will, Raje.'

Shivaji loved the expanse and elevation of the fort and its rugged, steep surroundings. The mountainous area had several small villages. Shivaji made friends with the village boys and staged mock battles with them. They respected him and enjoyed his company. They grew up together and soon became a part of Shivaji's regiment.

PRACHANDGAD OR TORNA FORT

During his mid-teens Shivaji was neither tall nor broad-shouldered. But his strong will and an insatiable appetite to establish an empire of his own made him stand out. He was determined to rid the land of the rule of the sultans and Mughals. His people were ever ready to stand by him.

Once in an argument with his father, Shivaji said, 'The need of the hour is to capture and possess as many forts as possible, Baba. That's the way to start building an empire. Forts will provide security and employment to the locals. The province around the forts can be brought under our control.'

Shahji was speechless with astonishment while Jijabai was thrilled by what a firebrand her son had become. There was no stopping Shivaji's enthusiasm now. His first target was the tall, mammoth hill fort of Prachandagad.

Shivaji's army was a spirited one. He trained them in the art of warfare, and how to be agile and swift-footed. They carried light weaponry, and knowing the lay of the land like the back of one's hand was an added advantage.

Sultan Adil Shah's men, who guarded the hill fort, were not very vigilant at the time Shivaji was planning to strike. They were confident that no one would dare to attack this massive fort that lay securely among the hills. Shivaji's surprise invasion caught them off guard.

The victory flag of Shivaji's nascent Maratha Empire was hoisted and his men rejoiced. Shivaji joined in the revelry. At the same time, he reminded them, 'Remember, my friends – the struggle has just begun. There are many more battles to be fought and as many forts to be captured.'

They all joined hands and circled the tower of the fort in the formation of a garland or *toran*, looked at the vast expanse of the region below and cried, 'We'll make this land our own! Glory be to Bhavani Devi!' The fort eventually came to be known as Torna.

VALOUR FORT OR PRATAPGARH

Shivaji's rapid capture of forts struck terror among the Muslim rulers. The furious Bijapur sultan stepped up his military strength. His spies reported that Shivaji had occupied the majestic Pratapgarh Fort and was defending it. The sultan was beside himself with rage. He turned to his general, Afzal

Khan, and said, 'How dare he! Does he think defeat and death cannot touch him? Prepare for attack, immediately! Take the largest army, the deadliest weapons we have and come back with him...dead or alive. The fort shall be ours.'

Afzal Khan, the dreaded seven-foot mountain of a man, led his formidable army to Pratapgarh. Shivaji's men saw the approaching army and looked anxiously at Shivaji, but their leader was calm. He told them not to worry and instructed his messenger, 'Go and tell the sultan's general that I'm ready for peace talks.'

Soon, a colourful *shamiana* was set up for the meeting between Afzal Khan and Shivaji in the plains below the fort. Afzal Khan was all set for the meeting. He had a dagger well hidden beneath his cloak. Shivaji too went prepared. He wore his armour underneath the silken kurta, and carried his metal tiger claws. He advised his army to stay alert.

The tall Khan came forward to embrace the shorter figure of Shivaji. In a blink, the embrace transformed into an iron grip and the dagger dug into Shivaji's back. However, when the dagger struck the armour it broke into two. Khan froze in confusion, and the very next moment, Shivaji's claws tore open Afzal Khan's abdomen. He screamed and tried to run, but it was too late... He dropped down dead.

The death of the general completely demoralized the sultan's army. Shivaji's men caught wind of what had happened and rushed forth to attack the sultan's soldiers from all directions. Cannons were fired and swords were wielded. The horses neighed in absolute terror. Many of the sultan's men were killed and some were imprisoned. The rest scattered and fled. The fort of Pratapgarh remained under Maratha control.

Shahji and Jijabai could not believe their ears.

'Afzal Khan killed? His army defeated by Shivaji? That's incredible! May Mahadev bless our son!' exclaimed Shahji. Jijabai said a silent prayer of thanks to Ma Bhavani and heaved a sigh of pride.

History rejoiced not only in recording Shivaji's victory but also in expressing his decency in treating the prisoners of war with honour and sympathy.

SINHAGAD OR LION FORT

Shivaji's empire building was at its height. His army was capturing forts left, right and centre. Some were lost and later recaptured. The Maratha Empire was growing steadily.

One day, he was at the Pratapgarh palace with his mother, playing a game of dice. As Jijabai was a more skillful player, Shivaji lost the game.

'What is my prize for winning?' asked Jijabai with a smile.

'Anything you wish, Aai,' Shivaji replied generously.

'Then get me that fort,' she said, promptly pointing to Kondhana Fort that lay across, bordering the horizon. For once, Shivaji was uncertain. He knew that this fort had been recently strengthened against attacks by the Mughals. He had not, so far, dared to recapture it. It had steep, high walls that were completely smooth. There was not a crack or crevice that could be used for foothold. Climbing the walls and entering the fort would be next to impossible. Also, the firing holes in the fort were invisible, which meant that there would be danger lurking in every corner. But Shivaji had to fulfil his mother's wishes.

Shivaji consulted his commandant, Tanaji, and both wracked their brains. After some time, suddenly, Shivaji smiled. Tanaji looked at him curiously.

'I just remembered Yeshwant,' Shivaji said.

'You mean our monitor lizard?' asked Tanaji

'Yes, I need you to feed him well and take him with you. Lead the army at the dead of night. Let the smallest of our men take ropes and cling on to Yeshwant's back. As the lizard climbs the vertical wall, so will our man carrying the ropes.'

Tanaji held his breath for one long moment and then said, 'Once Yeshwant reaches the top, our man will throw the rope down, and the rest of us will climb up!' The commandant could barely contain his excitement.

Shivaji patted his back and said, 'You've got it! Good luck. Get going and come back victorious.'

It was a dark, silent, chilly night. Tanaji and his men reached Kondhana Fort. Yeshwant the monitor lizard began to creep up the wall, steadily and noiselessly, while a young soldier, gripping one end of a rope, clung on to him for dear life. The rest of the men watched with bated breath from below. Time seemed to move ever so slowly. But once Yeshwant and his partner reached the top, action followed like lightning. The rope was secured on top by winding it around the fort's bastion. The soldiers used the other end of the rope to climb up and landed softly inside the fort. Not a soul was awake in the fort, except for the watchmen, who were promptly gagged and tied up by Tanaji's men.

At dawn, the fort was rudely woken up by the bold cries of Tanaji and his contingent, '*Har Har* Mahadev!'

By the time the enemy realized what was happening, Tanaji's army had their weapons on the ready. A fierce battle ensued, and by sunset, Tanaji's men hoisted the Maratha flag above the ramparts of the fort. They also lit a huge fire which soon burst into tall tongues of flame. The blaze of the fire of victory rose in the sky. Shivaji and his mother could witness the blaze and the flag of victory from Pratapgarh. Jijabai looked proudly at her son and said, 'Our men have won.' Shivaji smiled and bowed humbly.

Meanwhile, Tanaji was standing on the edge of the fort's steep wall, heaving a triumphant sigh. All of a sudden, someone attacked from behind him and killed him.

The troop returned to Pratapgarh with a heavy heart. Shivaji wondered why they were not jubilant. At the same time, his eyes searched for Tanaji; he couldn't wait to embrace him. But when the men told him about Tanaji, with tears streaming down their faces, there was a moment of painful silence. Heartbroken, Shivaji exclaimed with profound grief, 'I've won the Lion Fort, but I have lost my lion.'

In honour of Tanaji, Shivaji renamed the fort and it came to be known as Sinhagad.

CORONATION AT RAIGAD FORT

Many more battles were fought, and several more forts were captured over the next few years. History sighed as she struggled to keep count.

Shivaji was now the uncrowned king of the Maratha Empire.

Jijabai told him, 'Raje, you are now the supreme king and lord of the empire. I want to see a coronation ceremony performed for you. You shall be known as Chhatrapati Shivaji, the wise emperor who is an umbrella of protection for his people.'

The splendorous ceremony took place in the grand durbar of the fort of Raigad, the empire's capital. The throne was an opulent masterpiece studded with jewels resting on a column of gold. A priest from the holy city of Varanasi came specially to perform the sacred rituals. There were special prayers and offerings made to Ma Bhavani. Chhatrapati Shivaji mounted the throne to the sound of a booming gun salute. He was crowned with a brocade turban that had jewelled tassels. He held a pearl-studded gold umbrella while the people cheered, 'Long live our beloved Chattrapati Shivaji Maharaj!'

Chhatrapati Shivaji prostrated before his mother and took her blessings, and then, with his hands folded, he bowed in front of the garlanded picture of his father. Then, he mounted an elephant decked up in rich coverings and led a grand procession. The sun shone in all his glory while the soldiers clanged their spears on their shields and the people continued to cheer till their throats went hoarse.

Chhatrapati Shivaji was weighed, and precious metals, jewels, spices, wine, fruit and brocade worth his weight were distributed amongst the people. The celebrations ended gloriously at night with the full moon showering her good wishes on the emperor and his subjects.

OF KEBABS AND NAWABS

Awadh (present-day Lucknow area), ruled by the nawabs from the 14th to 17th century, was known for its exclusive cuisine, lavish splendour and unique monuments. Historians believe that minced meat wonders or kebabs were relished by the nawabs. When Nawab Asaf-ud-Daula was in power, loss of teeth due to ageing made him ask for the softest of kebabs. And so were born the melt-in-the mouth kebabs that visitors to Lucknow can enjoy even today. The nawab was fond of constructing artistic buildings and fashioning attractive gardens. He was immensely generous and charitable too. Monuments like the Imambara stand proof to this aspect of his personality.

Nawab Asaf-ud-Daula's bedroom was luxurious. The delicate curtains rustled softly in the morning breeze as day dawned and birds began to chirp. The nawab turned in his bed, threw aside his velvet quilt and woke up when the birds chirped louder, and a crow cawed noisily. He stepped out of his dream world and sat up on the bed. His feathery soft bed sank a little as he heaved himself out of it. The nawab flung back the lace curtains, opened the windows wide and took a deep breath of the cool morning air. He watched the birds fly hither and thither. Soon, he too would get as busy as the birds.

Bathing was an enjoyable activity for the nawab. He spent an hour in the hammam and came out refreshed. His personal valet was standing outside the bath, all set to help him with his attire. The nawab loved fine clothes and accessories. An exquisitely embossed, white, silken kurta with long, loose sleeves was his favourite garment. The valet helped him to put it on. He then wore a short pearl necklace and a longer one of pearl and sapphire, an armlet of gold and a bejewelled red turban.

The valet's skillful fingers groomed the nawab's long, drooping moustache. It went well with his dreamy eyes. He looked at his image in the mirror and adjusted his turban. Then he asked his valet to bring him his rings. He wore a ring on every finger of his left hand and a big ruby ring on his right thumb. The final touch was a dash of attar, delicately dabbed on the inside of his wrists.

The maid brought him a tall silver glass filled with pomegranate juice, which he relished.

Now the nawab was ready for his morning walk. He loved his rose garden. Roses of many hues were in bloom, and he drank in their beauty as he strolled around instructing the gardeners about watering, weeding, soil care and pruning. A brisk walk was not on his agenda, though it would do him good to reduce his bulk. He did not care about his weight.

The clear blue sky drew his attention, and he noticed a lone kite gliding across. It took him back to his youth when he used to be a keen kite flyer. He made up his mind to arrange for a kite-flying contest soon. What a lot of fun it would be!

A parrot pecking at a ripe guava on a tree reminded him of breakfast, and he returned to the palace. Saving his appetite for lunch, he had a light breakfast. The lavish array of food on the lunch table was what he always looked forward to.

The nawab met the ministers and assigned them their duties for the day as quickly as possible. His mind was on the dance performance he would be watching very soon. He walked faster than usual through the long corridors to reach the dance hall.

The hall resonated with lively music as he entered and settled on the royal divan. His eyes searched for his silver paandaan that usually lay on an ivory table next to the diwan. He drew the table closer and leaned back on the velvety cushions, resting his arms on the soft, richly covered bolsters. He gestured for the performance to start.

With unblinking eyes, he watched the dancers swirl in their gorgeous skirts and glide like apsaras on the stage in sync with the music.

'Wah! Wah!' said the nawab, his mouth filled with paan.

As the performance drew to a close, the kitchen staff were alerted. An army of chefs, cooks and servers rushed between the kitchen and the royal dining hall to get everything in order. A wide variety of vegetables, salads, meats, rotis, rice dishes and desserts were displayed attractively in dazzling silverware on the dining table, each item placed in its rightful place. Tall silver glasses were filled with flavourful fruit juices and placed next to each of the square-shaped silver plates.

The nawab arrived with his family and took his seat at the head of the table. He preferred to eat with his fingers and in silence. Cutlery would steal the taste of the food and talking would take his concentration away from it. Kebabs were his favourite item on the table. The specially prepared, crunchy, chewy kebabs were served to him ceremoniously by the head chef himself. The nawab took a big bite of it and had hardly begun chewing when everyone heard him cry out, 'Ouch!'

Everyone stopped eating and there was pin-drop silence all around. Only the nawab's wife, who was sitting close to him, muttered, 'The tobacco he keeps chewing has spoilt his teeth. I bet the kebab has broken a couple of his teeth!'

The nawab got up holding his jaw and left the dining hall. The others looked at each other and followed suit, while the kitchen staff started clearing the table.

The following day, the nawab summoned the head chef and commanded, 'From now on, I want kebabs to be so soft that they melt in my mouth.' He paused for a second and then added, 'Also, let it be known that the softest kebabs will receive royal patronage. I am giving a week's time for such kebabs to be presented to me.'

The chef's head began to reel. Traditionally, kebabs were supposed to be chewy and crunchy. But now the nawab wanted to set up a new tradition! The chef did not dare to say anything. He just bowed deeply and left.

The cooks swung into action. They worked day and night experimenting with new techniques to make soft kebabs.

News of the nawab's announcement of royal patronage for the softest kebabs reached the shop of the one-armed kebab expert, Tunde. He was excited to hear this news. Formerly known as Murad Ali, he was a passionate kite flyer who broke his arm while flying a kite from his terrace. One-armed kite-flying was not possible but making kebabs was. So, he assisted his father in making kebabs in his shop. After his father's death, Murad took over the business. Eventually, Murad Ali came to be known as Tunde, or the Armless One. Determined to win the nawab's patronage, he employed a host of men and women to grind and mix aromatic varieties of spices to be used in the kebabs. He supervised his assistants as they prepared the kebabs and administered the final expert touch to the dish.

After a week, the royal kebab makers were ready with their softer-than-the-softest kebabs and the nawab began to taste them one by one. The melt-in-the-mouth *galouti* kebab was about to be declared as the winner when Tunde presented his tender wonder, *tunde* kebab. One bite of it and the nawab declared it to be the best of all. With the delicious *tunde* kekab on the menu, the nawab began to relish his lunch like never before.

The hot summer months were ending and the fields awaited the seasonal rains. However, the days continued to be hot and dry. The kingdom was hit by a severe drought and food became scarce and expensive. The palace did not go hungry, but the rest of the kingdom did. The men were jobless, and their families were starving. The nawab was worried. He could not stand to see his people suffer and decided to do something about it. He called a meeting with his ministers and consulted them. None of their replies satisfied him. Then, he came up with a solution on his own.

The nawab summoned the best of architects and asked them to design a building that would be the pride of Awadh. *Why a building in these difficult times?* the people wondered. Nevertheless, the construction began. All the men of the kingdom were employed to raise the massive structure and were paid well for the work they did. Now, they could buy essential items even though they were costly.

The nawab watched the men at work. He was pleased with the effort they were putting in. But suddenly his eyes narrowed and a deep frown appeared between his eyebrows.

Now what? thought the ministers.

The nawab told them, 'I can't let these workers go hungry the whole day long. We must provide them with lunch.'

The ministers looked at each other.

The nawab smiled. 'Go and get our cooks. Ask them to prepare an all-in-one, easy-to-serve dish that can be distributed to the workers at lunchtime.'

The ministers hastened to implement the nawab's orders. The cooks got busy thinking up this new dish. Rice is easy to cook, they thought. But rice alone would not do... What about rice and meat? Adding some vegetables would make it complete. A sprinkling of spices would make it even tastier!

In a huge, heavy-bottomed cooking pot, the cooks put all these ingredients with enough water, placed it on a slow fire and covered the mouth of the pot. The rice along with the other ingredients began to cook in its own steam. The breeze carried the aroma of the dish right up to the palace and into

the nawab's chamber. The nawab was caught off guard. He shook his head and inhaled deeply. He summoned the cooks at once.

'What is this extremely delicious dish that you are cooking?' asked the nawab.

The cooks explained what it was. The nawab lost no time in pronouncing, 'This dish too shall enter the royal kitchen. Henceforth, it shall be presented on the lunch table. Call it by whatever name you want.' The amused cooks nodded and left.

Now the cooks were doubly loaded with the job of cooking the dish, which they decided to call biryani, both for the workers as well as for the royal family. But they did not mind the work. They made it extra special for the nawab with more ghee and spices. They knew he loved and appreciated good food.

Biryani satisfied everyone's palate in the kingdom. The workers ate well and worked well. They were allowed to take some biryani for their families too.

The building was completed to the satisfaction of the nawab, and he was happy that he was able to lessen the suffering of his subjects. He began to enjoy his share of the super-soft kebabs and tasty biryani. So did the rest of the royal family. The kitchen staff too got a good helping of both.

THE QUEEN WHO DARED

The present-day districts of Ramanathapuram and Sivagangai in the state of Tamil Nadu had independent rulers since the 17th century. They were known for their military prowess. The female rulers bore the title of Nachiyar. Velu Nachiyar fought and triumphed against the British after her husband was killed in a skirmish. She stayed in hiding, changing base frequently to dodge the British. With the support of Hyder Ali, sultan of the kingdom of Mysore (now Mysuru), she built a powerful army that included many valiant women. The army attacked the British in a brilliantly planned rebellion. Commander-in-chief Kuyili gave up her life willingly, making the supreme sacrifice to uphold the sovereignty of her land. A postage stamp was released by the government of India in Velu Nachiyar's honour in 2008, and her memorial was inaugurated in Sivagangai in 2014.

From time to time, performances are staged on the life and achievements of Velu Nachiyar in various parts of Tamil Nadu. People love to watch these shows.

Every corner of the small kingdom of Ramanathapuram was rejoicing. So much so that the old lady who lay curled up in a corner of her little home came out to see what the fuss was about.

'Hmmph...so much celebration for a girl,' she grimaced when she came to know that the queen had given birth to a girl child.

A neighbour informed her, 'Our king and queen are very happy. They do not think girls are inferior to boys in any way.'

The old woman frowned but did not say anything more.

The queen named her daughter Velu. The proud parents watched the baby turn, crawl, sit up, toddle and lisp. Velu grew up to be a bright and lively child. Soon, it was time for her to start school. After a brief prayer to the goddess of learning, her parents put her under the care and guidance of many able teachers. Velu was an excellent student. She learnt horse riding with as much enthusiasm as archery. She could wield the sword and the stick with equal ease.

Velu, however, preferred martial arts to everything else. Her agilty amazed her tutors. She was equally interested in reading and writing and had a great love for her mother tongue – Tamil.

Her mornings were usually spent in horse-riding practice and other outdoor lessons. After that she would stride back to the palace, ravenous.

'What's for lunch, Amma?' she would ask eagerly. Her favourite dish was chunks of heavily spiced potatoes with dollops of yoghurt.

Velu would then run for her classroom lessons. She liked learning foreign languages the best. Her tutors taught her Urdu and French. She wished to learn Latin too, but there was no one who could teach it to her.

Velu's parents decided that sixteen was the right age for marriage. When Velu set eyes on the accomplished prince of Sivagangai kingdom, Udaithevar, the man chosen by her parents, she too liked the idea of getting married.

The wedding was a grand four-day affair. After the celebrations had died down,Thevar asked his new bride, 'Let's get away for a few days. Where do you want to go?'

'How about a temple tour?'

And so, off they went visiting temples big and small in both their kingdoms. They made generous offerings and invoked the blessings of the residing deities so they could rule justly.

Thevar admired Velu's wit and wisdom. He was amused to hear her speak in French. He looked on in awe when Velu opened her Urdu book and read it backwards from the last page.

'I'm not here to entertain you with my talents,' Velu would say in mock anger.

After a while, Thevar's father retired from his kingly duties and left on a pilgrimage with his wife. The kingdom was now in the hands of Thevar and Velu. They proved to be good rulers. Thevar consulted Velu in the matters of policies of governance and honoured her advice. Under their joint leadership, the kingdom thrived.

When Princess Vellachi was born, Velu was over the moon. She sang lullabies to her daughter just as her mother used to sing to her. The princess began receiving the same training in warfare that Velu had got more than a decade ago. But life is never a smooth journey for royalty in any era. Vellachi was hardly ten when a whiff of a political tempest began to surface. Trouble started brewing with the arrival of the British East India Company. It did not take long for Thevar and Velu to become aware of its progressively looming presence. With mounting apprehension, they a kept watch over every move of the foreigners.

'They claim to be a trading company, but can you see that they have vested interests too? We should be very careful,' Velu said worriedly. Thevar agreed.

'Let's wait for them to make a move. We'll decide our plan of action depending on their motive,' Thevar said.

Their wait was not a long one. Things became tense in the domains of the local rulers as the British inched their way into their territories. They threatened them to surrender at gunpoint. Though the British did not have massive armies, their weaponry was modern and deadly. Any opposition was bound to prove fatal. All the little kingdoms of south India that had so far ruled their regions in peace and lived in harmony with one another began to dread the British. Most of them surrendered to their rule of law, including the nawab of Arcot who was one of the most influential rulers of the southern region. There were a few bravehearts who chose to oppose the British. Thevar was one of them. He prepared himself to face them in the battlefield and Velu was ready to support him.

'You take care of Vellachi,' he told her.

The British were caught by surprise. They had not expected the small kingdom of Sivagangai to resist them so boldly. The British general called for an emergency meeting. At the meeting, a plot was hatched, and the soldiers got ready to strike.

Pradosham was an important bimonthly event in all the Shiva temples in the kingdom. During sunset, special prayers and offerings were made to the deity. Thevar, an ardent devotee of Lord Shiva, never missed attending this puja at the main temple of Sivagangai. Dressed in a simple white dhoti with a *rudraksha* mala on his bare chest, he would go to the temple accompanied by several other devotees.

On one such day, when prayers and chants were in full swing, Thevar stood with hands folded and eyes closed in reverence, reciting mantras. Suddenly, gunshots were heard at close quarters. The devotees started running amuck as bullets whizzed by. There was utter chaos and commotion in the temple. One of the bullets hit Thevar's bare chest and he slumped to the ground at the feet of the deity. Soon, the temple was littered with bodies of the devotees who had fallen prey to the bullets. Having done their duty, the British soldiers retreated, leaving Sivagangai in a state of shock.

When Velu heard this news, she froze in utter disbelief. The following morning, Sivagangai was bathed in bright sunlight. But when Velu stepped out of her home, she glowed brighter with the fire that scorched the depths of her heart. She was determined to avenge her husband's death and resolved to free her kingdom from the clutches of the British. Rani Velu Nachiyar was eager to tackle and overpower her treacherous foe. But her inner voice cautioned her. 'Your purpose is powerful. But to face the British and vanquish them, each member of your army must be as strong as you are. Facing the British in a head-on battle will not be easy.' Velu bowed to the guiding spirit of her late husband and decided to lay low till the time was right.

Queen Velu entrusted Princess Vellachi's care to a close friend.

'I may be absent for a long period of time as I have a deadly enemy to vanquish,' she said. Once her friend had assured her that the princess was in safe hands, Velu started planning her next move. The British could not be trifled with. They had lethal arms and ammunition in their possession. They were getting ready to take over the kingless kingdom of Sivagangai, while she was a fugitive queen with practically nothing more than an iron resolve in her possession. Much planning and deliberation were needed from her side. She needed support, military and otherwise.

Velu decided to get in touch with Sultan Hyder Ali of Mysore, who at that time was a force to be reckoned with in south India. She wrote him a humble letter in

Urdu, requesting a meeting with him. The sultan was more than happy to support the queen as he himself had been wanting to clip the wings of the British. So, he welcomed Velu Nachiyar as he would a long-lost friend.

'You speak the language of friendship,' he told her. 'Tell me – how can I assist you.?'

Much to the sultan's amazement, Velu spoke to him at length in fluent Urdu.

Hyder Ali liked her unwavering resolve to overthrow the British. He offered her arms, soldiers and expenses to achieve her purpose, and promised to be her ally and give her every kind of support to face a common enemy. At the same time, he cautioned her, 'You must be very careful at every step. The British forces are exceedingly strong. Take your time to plan your strategy. Gather your forces and ensure that they are confident enough to face the enemy and will support you to the very end.'

Velu took his advice in the right spirit. She chose a team of brave young women, motivated them to fight for their kingdom and trained them patiently in the art of warfare. All this took time. Everything had to be done undercover, without raising the suspicion of the British. Keeping Hyder Ali's words in mind, Velu worked steadily with single-minded determination.

Velu's favourite warrior was a woman named Kuyili.

'My mother is my role model,' she told Velu. 'Her life's journey has shown me that life is not worth living without courage.'

Velu made Kuyili the commander-in-chief of the women's army. She called her *veerathalapathy* – the bravest commander ever. Velu was now sure that with the help of her army of bravehearts, she could win the war.

Velu and her army were all set. When it was time to face the British, Velu and Kuyili plunged into action as per the singular strategy they had devised. It was a risky mission, but they were prepared to face the consequences, come what may. Their hearts swelling with positive energy, they proceeded.

It was the final day of Navaratri. The temple inside the fort of Sivagangai was open to all devotees on that day. Velu's female brigade made use of this occasion to enter the fort in the guise of devotees carrying big baskets of flower and fruit offerings to the goddess Rajarajeswari. Beneath their glamorous silken saris, they wore their armour, and under the flowers and fruits in the baskets their weapons lay hidden. When the festivities were at their height, the army struck. The silken saris were discarded. The flowers and fruits

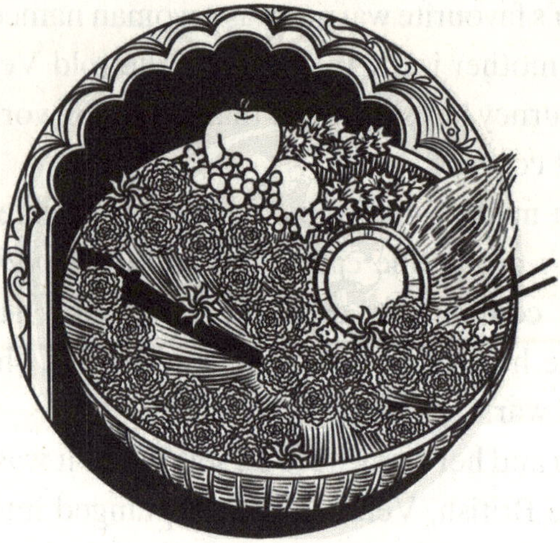

lay strewn on the ground. The women soldiers struck, wielding their weapons. The British forces that were keeping guard were caught unawares. Velu and her soldiers launched a fierce attack.

A bitter battle ensued. Meanwhile, Kuyili made her companions pour the oil meant for lighting the lamps on her. Then, she rushed into the armoury chambers of the British and set herself on fire. There was an ear-splitting noise as the arsenal exploded. The British lost their sophisticated arms to the fire while Velu lost her *veerathalapathy,* the bravest warrior to have walked their land. The British retreated. Kuyili's incredible sacrifice filled Velu's heavy heart with gratitude.

The war was won, and it was a defeat that was recorded in the history of the British East India

Company. Rani Velu Nachiyar fulfilled her vow and reclaimed her kingdom.

By now, Princess Vellachi had grown up to be a bright youngster. She was excited about meeting her mother. With the help of her foster mother, she arranged for a special function to welcome her mother and her brave army. The whole kingdom rejoiced, including the old woman who lay curled up in a corner of her little home. She could no longer get up. From her corner, she blessed Velu and all womenfolk.

Rani Velu Nachiyar's kingdom was once again a peaceful place to live in. It remained productive and progressive all through her reign. It continued to prosper even later when Princess Vellachi took over as the queen, until the course of history decided to take a different turn.

AN ODE TO A REBEL KING

India's struggle for freedom from British rule started when the British East India Company landed in the country in the 17th century under the guise of doing trade. Many Indian rulers began business transactions with them. One such ruler, the nawab of Arcot in south India, failed miserably and was steeped in debt. To clear his debts, the nawab allowed the East India Company to collect taxes from the areas under his domain. Kattabomman's region was a part of this domain, but he stubbornly refused to pay tax. The East India Company's attempt to capture him failed. He escaped and dodged the British forces for a long time, but was eventually caught, imprisoned and put on trial. False accusations were made and the judge sentenced him to be hanged. Kattabomman is admired as an unparalleled freedom fighter who died a heroic death.

Arumugathamma and her children stood on the moonlit terrace of their palace in Panchalankurichi in present-day Tirunelveli district of Tamil Nadu. The little ones loved listening to family stories and their mother was only too willing to tell them. Kattabomman was the eldest of the four children. That evening, Amma was telling them why their father called himself Aadi Kattabomman. 'He was the first from their clan to become the minister of the armed forces in the court of King Jagveera Pandyan. He was an efficient minister and very loyal to the king. So, when the time came, the king chose him as his heir because he had no children of his own.

'When your father was crowned, he was so proud to add Jagveera Pandya to the family name, Kattabomman. And that is how he came to be known – Jagveera Pandya Kattabomman.'

'So…so…we hav-v-e no r-r-oyal blood?' asked Kumarasamy, Kattabomman's brother.

'Don't ever say that. Royalty was bestowed upon us and that's an honour,' Kattabomman said.

'Tell us more, Amma,' said Kattabomman's youngest sister.

The queen continucd, 'Oncc, when your father went hunting, riding the royal steed like the wind, an unusual sight met his eye. He had gone deep into the forest with his courtiers and hunting dogs.'

'What happened then?' asked Kattabomman impatiently.

She smiled. 'He saw a tiny rabbit. But this little creature was so brave that when it was chased by the dogs, it turned round and faced them without a trace of fear in its eyes. Uncertain how to react, the dogs stood growling nervously, and the rabbit simply hopped away. The king was astonished. He got off his horse and reverentially touched the ground where the rabbit had stood.'

'"If even a rabbit of this soil can be this brave, it is clear that this land of ours breeds bravery," he exclaimed proudly. In that moment, he decided to build his fortress on that very spot...'

'The fort of Panchalankurichi!' Kattabomman yelled excitedly, interrupting his mother.

'Yes, my son,' said the queen. 'The fort is one of its kind. Its walls were built using black clay mixed with straw and paddy for extra strength. The thorny bushes surrounding it prevent intruders from entering our stronghold. The fort is resilient and capable of withstanding any kind of attack, you know.'

The clock tower chimed ten and Amma said, 'Time to go to bed, children. We leave for Tiruchendur tomorrow morning.'

'Oh, yes! To the seashore temple of Lord Murugan!' the young voices exclaimed joyously. The royal family was devoted to Lord Murugan, but frequent visits to the temple were not possible as it was about forty miles away from the palace.

Kattabomman went to bed with all sorts of thoughts floating around in his mind. He was in awe of his father's courage and fearlessness, and how deeply he cared about the welfare of his subjects. He remembered his father's words: 'My son, remember to enter the battlefield only for self-defence. It is our policy to live in peace and harmony with our neighbouring kings, as far as possible.'

While asleep at night, Kattabomman dreamt of fighting battles against those who tried to attack the kingdom, and during the day he fought mock battles with his brothers.

When Kattabomman was thirty years old, his father died. Kattabomman was crowned king. He proved to be a good administrator, just and kind. He not only strengthened Panchalankurichi Fort further and made it impregnable but also beautified it. Though his territory was small, comprising not more than thirty villages, Kattabomman was proud of his land and his people. He bore in mind his father's words and kept good relations with his neighbours.

Kattabomman was an early riser. He would have loved to visit Tiruchendur temple every day, but the distance was an inconvenience. So, with his hands folded above his head, he used to stand facing the direction of the temple and chant the Lord's name thrice loudly. He did this every morning and evening at the time when offerings were made to the deity at the temple. To ensure that he never missed the prayer time, he built forty bell towers all along the way from Tiruchendur to Panchalankurichi. The bells sounded one after another in quick succession at the time when offerings were made in the temple.

Full moon nights were joyous occasions in Panchalankurichi. Kattabomman would invite artistes both popular and lesser known, young and old, men

and women to perform in the palace. His sisters too danced and sang during these events. Then, after the festivities, there was a grand feast. Special offerings from Tiruchendur temple were arranged to be sent and distributed among the guests.

All was well till the British East India Company arrived. Trouble started brewing when they began to assert themselves as masters of the land. The day Kattabomman learnt that the Company had sailed into the port of Madras (now Chennai), built their fort there and assumed authority to levy heavy taxes from every kingdom of the region, his blood boiled.

'Pay tax to a foreigner for our own land? How ridiculous! I will not pay a single paisa!' he cried. The neighbouring kings preferred to let the British have their way. They knew they couldn't match the British in strength, and disobedience would only lead to disaster. Cowardice got the better of them, and they allied with the British for their own security.

'Don't be defiant! Don't you see how strong the foreigners are? They'll take our land and throw us out, maybe even kill us, if we refuse to pay the tax.' The neighbouring kings tried reasoning with Kattabomman, but he turned a deaf ear to them and openly declared his dislike for the British.

Kattabomman's brothers and his two generals began to wonder if he was being brave or foolhardy.

'The foreigners are sure to be angry with our king. What do you think they will do to him? What will happen to us?' the villagers talked amongst themselves. There was an atmosphere of fear and in the kingdom. Kattabomman knew that his rebellious attitude would provoke the British to take drastic steps, but he was prepared to face their fury. He prayed sincerely to Lord Murugan to help him protect his land and his people. He decided he was not going to give in under any circumstances.

'There is no time to waste. We must prepare for war. The British may attack us at any time,' he told his men. The people were astonished at the courage of his convictions. Later, Kattabomman came to be known as Veera Pandya Kattabomman – the courageous Pandya.

The war preparations began in earnest. In the meantime, Kattabomman pacified the worried villagers. 'Have no fear… No harm will come to you,' he told them. 'Our army is strong and it will defend our land. Let us pray to Lord Murugan for his protection.'

For a few days, nothing untoward happened.

'The British are busy strategizing, I suppose,' said his brother, Oomaithurai.

'Let them plan. We are ready to face them, are we not?' retorted Kattabomman.

On the sixth day after Deepavali, there was the annual temple festival at Tiruchendur. Kattabomman went to attend it along with his family. The British major general learnt of this and took advantage of the situation – he lay in ambush for Kattabomman.

However, just before proceeding to attack, the general thought of giving Kattabomman one last chance. He sent word to him asking him to surrender unconditionally to save his skin and his kingdom.

How would the king react to the threat? everyone wondered. True to his nature, Kattabomman acted boldly. He read out his reply to his people before sending it to the British general. The letter said:

> *We are sons of the soil. We live with honour and dignity. We do not bow to foreigners who want to rule us. We shall fight if necessary and we will win.*

As soon as the British general got the message, he commanded, 'Launch the attack at once and bring Kattabomman to me!'

War broke out. Kattabomman led his army to face the British soldiers and fought valiantly. The British were unable to match Kattabomman's skill in warfare. Soon, they were completely overwhelmed and withdrew. The people of Panchalankurichi breathed a sigh of relief, thinking that the worst was over. But Kattabomman was wiser.

'Do you think the British will leave us in peace?' He was laughing as he looked at his brothers and the chieftain. 'No. They will never rest until they make me bow to them, and that's not going to happen. I will bow only to Lord Murugan.'

'Does that mean we're going to war again?' asked his chieftain.

Kattabomman nodded. 'Yes, and this time, I am sure they will come with their cannons.'

'But the fort cannot stand the onslaught of that deadly weapon,' said the chieftain.

'I know,' replied Kattabomman.

'So...'

'So we will leave. Let the empty fort take the bombardment of the cannonballs. If we can save ourselves, we can always rebuild it later.'

The fort was evacuated quickly. Kattabomman arranged for his family and others to stay safely elsewhere. It was decided that he and his brothers would leave in the dead of night and disappear into the depths of the surrounding jungle.

Soon, the sound of the British guns rent the air. Kattabomman and his brothers remained in hiding for days, surviving on wild berries and water from streams. Sometimes, a loyal villager would bring them some food.

It was not easy for the British army to enter the fort. It stood strong.

The British general commanded, 'Attack at the corners!' The cannons were moved to face the corners and when they blasted, the fort gave way, but Kattabomman was nowhere to be found.

The general was beside himself with fury. 'Has he run away? Does he think he can outsmart me? Well...he has a bitter lesson to learn.' Furious, the general sent his men out in all directions to hunt for Kattabomman.

The British soldiers found it difficult to advance in the unknown forest area. Kattabomman and his men were able to dodge them with ease for they knew every inch of the land. The British general was losing his patience. He realized that if he wanted to capture Kattabomman, he would have to change his tactics. So, he approached the king of Pudukkottai – a neighbouring kingdom of Panchalankurichi – who had become his ally. The general persuaded the king to get Kattabomman to his palace on the pretext of giving him asylum. Once Kattabomman was in Pudukkottai, he could be handed over to the British. The king agreed to the arrangement.

As per the plan, the king of Pudukkottai offered asylum to Kattabomman. Failing to recognize the king's treachery, Kattabomman accepted his invitation and entered the Pudukkottai palace. Within seconds, he was captured by British soldiers.

'Beg for pardon and you shall be set free,' said the British general to Kattabomman.

'Set free to do what? Pay taxes and bow down to you? You call that freedom?' asked Kattabomman, enraged.

'I will have you hanged from the nearest tree if you do not ask for mercy,' the general snarled.

'Do what you want,' Kattabomman replied, undaunted.

'In that case…hang him!' the general yelled, loud and clear for all to hear.

Dogs howled and the sky darkened as the hangman led Kattabomman to a tamarind tree outside the palace walls. Lightning flashed and a thunderstorm broke out. Mother Nature paid ode to Veera Pandya Kattabomman. A pall of gloom descended over Panchalankurichi, where the tearful villagers prayed for the departing soul. The bells of Tiruchendur temple chimed, and Lord Murugan missed the voice of his devotee calling out his name. In that moment, the country witnessed the beginnings of a rebellion against British supremacy and history recorded it.

MONARCH OF MEN AND MELODY

Swati Thirunal was the maharaja of the princely state of Travancore in Kerala from 1829 to 1846. Posterity will remember the maharaja as a person of astounding intelligence and artistic acumen. Having composed more than 400 songs in both Carnatic and Hindustani styles, he was a musical genius who occupies an important place in the history of Indian music. To this day, his songs are played in concert halls. Swati Thirunal was also a ruler and administrator par excellence. The prosperous state of Travancore was a testimony to his progressive measures and reforms.

The royal priest declared the day as a *thiru-nal*, meaning 'an auspicious day'. The star of the day, Swati, was on the rise, which meant it would be beneficial for those born on the day. Despite this, there was an atmosphere of tension within the palace as well as outside amongst the people of Travancore; the summer heat of April only added to this feeling of unease. Then, not too long afterwards, nervousness gave way to delight. The midwife peeped out from the first-floor window of the palace and announced, 'The queen has given birth to a boy! Mother and child are well.'

The tension that had shrouded Travancore earlier was because of the increasing interference of the British in the kingdom's administration. According to their annexation policy, if there was no male heir to the throne of a princely state, the kingdom would come under them. Gowri Laxmi Bayi, the reigning queen of Travancore, had no sons. What would happen to the kingdom? The queen prayed fervently day and night as did everyone else. Their prayers were partially answered when the queen was finally with child. But would she give birth to a boy or a girl? There were mixed feelings of joy and doubt. The royal family made special offerings of food and wealth at the family temple of Lord Padmanabha and then distributed them amongst the people.

Much to everyone's relief, the queen gave birth to a boy. There was a unparalleled jubilation in the kingdom. While the people rejoiced, the child cried and continued to wail even after his mother fed him. The queen laid him in his cradle, patted him and gently rocked him to and fro. Still, he cried. Suddenly, the strains of a soft, melodious lullaby drifted into the chamber. It was a lilting tune that could put any child to sleep. A male voice sang: 'Are you the little darling of the cool moon, or are you the beautiful lotus flower, or the pretty parrot or the dancing peacock…'

The child stopped crying. His big eyes followed his maternal uncle as he walked up to the cradle, singing the song. He continued to sing till the child's eyelids drooped and he fell asleep.

The naming ceremony of the heir was a quiet affair. The family priest anointed the child while the astrologer declared that the little one had an extraordinarily rich horoscope. The child would be remembered for all ages as a great king of the Chera dynasty. According to the family tradition, he was named after the star that represented the day he was born, and so he came to be known as Swati Thirunal. Just as the ceremony was concluding, there was a commotion outside the palace. The queen left the child with her sister and went to see what the matter was.

'Your Majesty! A white elephant has fallen into our jungle trap,' said one of the men who was standing outside.

'Oh! Is the elephant safe?' asked Queen Gowri.

'Yes, yes. He is safe and well.'

The queen gave them a curious look and let them continue. The person who had come forward to speak was the caretaker of the forest area.

He said, 'Your Majesty, according to our beliefs, this is an auspicious omen. The white elephant is a rare creature. Its appearance on this day indicates the greatness of our future king. Can I bring him here to meet our beloved prince?'

The queen nodded her approval.

The majestic elephant walked up to the palace gates. The queen's sister came out carrying little prince Swati in her arms. The elephant laid his trunk on the child's forehead gently as if it was blessing him. The queen got a basketful of bananas for the elephant to eat and a pot of silver coins for the mahout of the pachyderm.

The crowd cried, 'Long live our future king! Hail to the royal family!'

Meanwhile, the British were not sitting back and relaxing. They were still focussed on the Travancore kingdom. They sent word to the queen, 'Since a male heir is born, he shall be the ruler henceforth. The queen must step down.'

Queen Gowri was shocked. Swati was all of four months. But there was no way she could defy the British – the foreigners had grown too powerful.

It was the monsoon season. The sky was overcast, and the rain poured heavily. But the weather was the last thing on the royal family's mind. Four-month-old Swati was seated on the throne. He wore a mini bejewelled turban for a crown and was dressed in the smallest ever golden velvet royal robe! His tiny fingers were wrapped around a little sword in a black velveteen sheath. History was amused to record this scene.

Queen Gowri Laxmi Bayi sat beside her son on the throne of the regent. But, more often than not, the king sat on his mother's lap while she met with the council of ministers. At other times, his aunt, Parvati, took him away to feed him and put him to sleep while the queen continued with her administrative work.

Unfortunately, King Swati was able to enjoy the comfort of his mother's presence for only two years. Travancore was steeped in sorrow at Queen Gowri Laxmi Bayi's untimely death. Parvati Bayi took over as queen-regent, and she also looked after her nephew with love and care. She would wake up very early in the morning and tend to all his needs before her duties as queen-regent would begin for the day.

Time passed by. Days became months and months became years. One morning, even before the birds began to chirp, Parvati woke up to the sweet sound of music. It was four-year-old Swati singing: 'Are you the little darling of the cool moon, or are you the beautiful lotus flower…'

Parvati was wonderstruck. The little boy was on the terrace, looking at the gibbous moon, lost in the song.

She ran up to him, gathered him in his arms and asked, 'How did you learn this song?'

Swati laughed and said, 'Why, you, Amma and Ammavan have sung it to me so often!'

Parvati was speechless. 'He's singing it in perfect tune. He is naturally gifted,' she said to herself, her heart heaving with pride.

'Do you want to learn music, Swati?' she asked him.

Swati jumped up and gave her a hug. 'Yes, Cheriamma,' he whispered in her ears.

'But remember, Swati. You are Maharaja Swati Thirunal Rama Varma. While it would be wonderful to be a musician, your kingly duties must come first.'

'I understand,' Swati said and ran away, continuing to hum the lullaby.

Parvati got the best tutors to teach Swati all that he needed to learn to perform his kingly duties. His favourite subjects were mathematics and science. He loved his mother tongue, Malayalam, but he became well versed in other languages too. In less than a decade, he learnt Telugu, Kannada, Marathi, Tamil and Sanskrit. Parvati saw to it that he learnt English as well because it was needed while interacting with the British. Swati also picked up Persian and Hindustani, which would be useful to keep in touch with the northern states, be it in war or peace.

One day, when Swati was in his early teens, he picked up his slate and pencil and sketched the forty-seventh Euclidean proposition, which is also known as the Pythagoras theorem. He turned the slate around for his tutor to see if he had sketched it properly.

'Very good, son. You've drawn the theorem perfectly. Not everybody can do it so well.'

'This is geometry, right?' Swati asked.

The tutor nodded.

'I'll call it *jyamiti*,' said Swati. Seeing the puzzled expression on the tutor's face, he laughed. 'Today in Sanskrit class, I learnt that the word geometry is derived from the Sanskrit root word *jyamiti*. Other mathematical terms like hexagon, heptagon and so on are also derived from Sanskrit.'

The tutor nodded in wonder. 'You're right. Very few people know this.'

Parvati was very pleased with young Swati's progress. Another couple of years and he would be formally crowned king at the age of sixteen. She was also proud of his budding musical and literary genius. His language teachers were amazed at the imagery and depth of his poetry.

Music in the kingdom of Travancore was gaining momentum under the tutelage of several renowned musicians. Swati effortlessly learnt the basics of ragas (tunes), talas (rhythm) and *laya* (tempo) of the songs. He put in hours of practice to perfect his singing.

One morning, as usual, Swati was practising music on the terrace. However, the song sounded different that day. Parvati noticed that it was more melodious, more soothing and more divine. She came up to him and asked, 'Who taught you this song, son?'

'No one, Cheriamma,' Swati replied casually.

'Then how are you singing it?' she asked curiously.

Swati laughed and replied, 'It just came to me. The melody and pattern took shape in my heart and the song flowed.'

'May Lord Padmanabha bless him,' Parvati said to herself, taking pride in her nephew's talent.

Swati Thirunal merged into the ocean of music. A deep creative sense coloured each phrase of his every song. He had moved beyond the process of being tutored. At the same time, he preserved his guru's advice in the depths of his heart.

'My son,' his guru had told him. 'Every night, before you sleep, hum the song that circles in your mind. Keep thinking of it till you fall asleep. In the morning, the song will come alive and flow smoothly from your vocal cords.'

Swati Thirunal the king became known as an outstanding composer of divine songs in the classical style. Musical giants from all over flocked to Travancore to meet him. He became a great patron of not only music but also literature and other art forms.

The people of Travancore were proud of their talented ruler, but there were some who did not approve of his musical ways. The two opposing sides often got into debates.

One day, during one such debate, a non-supporter said, 'No doubt he is a great musician and a greater patron of the arts. But music and art don't make a monarch...'

'I agree. The kingdom cannot be neglected at the cost of music!' said another.

The supporters rushed to their king's defence. 'He does what any good ruler would do. He works to keep us happy. Our economy, agriculture and trade are flourishing!' said one of them.

'True. He is not ostentatious. He is generous and kind, and look what he has done for education. Built schools for free education and set up libraries to create an interest in learning,' said another.

'A king with high principles! He has always believed in peace, not war. And have you seen the observatory that he has built?' They kept singing his praises, and soon, those who came to scorn began to nod in assent.

One loud voice proclaimed, 'He is every inch a maharaja as well as a melody king. I can still recall his words at the inaugural speech of last year's Navaratri festival at the new temple. He said, "As a king, I strive to do my duty to keep my people happy and well. At the same time, we need the grace of God for our well-being".' The annual Navaratri festival was a special occasion in Travancore. Mellifluous melodies filled the air, and dances were performed all through the nine days of the festival. The king gave generous gifts to the performers and donated large sums of money to temples.

However, history could keep up this happy state of affairs for just over another decade. Then, she began to change her course, bringing new twists and turns. When a new British Resident for Travancore was appointed, the dice became loaded against Swati Thirunal. With the new Resident taking charge, policies changed and corruption crept into the administration. The king was made to watch helplessly, with less and less say in matters of governance. His judgment was bypassed while corrupt officials took unreasonable decisions. The people, of course, suffered.

This agonizing situation began to tell on the king's health. Fervent prayers for his well-being echoed from every corner of the kingdom, but his hour of departure chimed loud and clear. Maharaja Swati Thirunal passed away at the age of thirty-three.

Fire devoured Swati Thirunal's bodily remains, but it could not destroy his legacy. Not only is he remembered as a well-loved and respected king of the Chera dynasty but also as a musical legend for his sacred compositions in Carnatic and Hindustani music. His songs are popular amongst musicians, both young and old, in the country and abroad. Even the lullaby that he loved is sung not only by mothers for their little ones but also by musicians.

THE QUEEN-REGENT

Maharaja Ranjit Singh was a powerful king who united the warring chieftains of Punjab and established a mighty empire in the early 19th century. He chose a beautiful young girl, Jind Kaur, to be his wife, even though she was not from a royal family. Known as Rani Jindan, she proved herself to be remarkable. She ruled the kingdom of Punjab as regent to her minor son, Dalip. She managed to resist the encroachment of the British into Punjab for a few years. But, eventually, she was forced to surrender to their might. Rani Jindan carved her niche in the annals of history as an incredibly courageous woman with an unconquerable will. She is remembered as a queen who loved her kingdom and her people more than herself.

Jind Kaur was the daughter of a kennel keeper in the service of Maharaja Ranjit Singh of Punjab.

Her sparkling eyes and sharp features attracted the attention of the maharaja.

Young Jindan was flattered as well as apprehensive when the maharaja wanted to get to know her. Eventually, he expressed his wish to marry her.

Their wedding was a simple affair.

The royal couple loved and respected each other. Jindan admired Ranjit Singh's leadership skills and learnt about kingship from him. Ranjit Singh, on the other hand, was pleased and delighted with her intelligence and smartness.

'Maybe you could rule Punjab better than me,' he would say to tease her.

Unfortunately, their relationship lasted only four years. The untimely death of Ranjit Singh left Jindan Kaur widowed at the age of twenty-two.

Their son, Dalip, was just over a year old when Ranjit Singh died. Jindan was his last wife and that put Dalip way down in the line of succession. He had several stepbrothers who were older than him. They were the sons of the senior wives of Ranjit Singh, who had a right to the throne more than Dalip had.

Jindan raised Dalip with a lot of love and care. She believed that as Prince Dalip Singh, the boy would live up to his father's ideals. Then, in four years' time, there was yet another unexpected turn of events that changed their lives.

Jindan was in her bedchamber with five-year-old Dalip. It was his bedtime. Every night, he went to sleep listening to his mother tell stories about the valour and virtue of the Sikh gurus. It was at this time that news of the recent happenings in the kingdom reached her ears. It looked like her son was destined for fame. The line of succession had suddenly been cleared for Dalip to become king. She pinched herself to make sure she was not dreaming. She knew she was awake and that meant the news was true.

Jindan was aware of the strife that had been going on within the royal family of late. Ranjit Singh's older sons fought for the throne, using foul means. There was treachery and murder. One after another, all the successors had fallen to the sword, leaving the throne vacant for Dalip.

How can a five-year-old be king? thought Jindan.

'But why not? I, his mother, will be there by his side as the queen-regent till he comes of age,' she said to herself.

Lying down beside her son that night, Jindan's mind took a trip down memory lane. She remembered how much her husband loved the company of their son. He had chosen the name, Dalip, for the child and wished him to be wise and just. He used to love holding baby Dalip and thanking Waheguru for the bundle of joy.

'The name Dalip means king, you know,' he had told Jindan once, winking with his one good eye as he smiled.

'If you say so, sarkar.' She addressed him fondly and respectfully as 'sarkar'. Jindan wondered whether her son would become king.

But strange are the ways of Waheguru, Jindan thought looking at her son sleeping peacefully. She also remembered with a shudder the astrologer's prediction at the time of his birth:

> *'He is born at an inauspicious hour. He will acquire name and fame but will lose them soon.'*

She could see the first part of it was coming true. But…the second part…would that come true also? No. She didn't want to believe it.

'Who says predictions are always correct?' she asked herself. She kissed her son softly and tried to catch some sleep. The next few days were going to be hectic.

Maharaja Dalip Singh was robed in resplendent red for the coronation. Rani Jindan Kaur was dressed in plain white. A string of pearls adorned her neck and a delicate gossamer veil tried to hide her beautiful face.

Dalip paid obeisance to the holy text – the Guru Granth Sahib. He then reverentially bowed in front of the priest and accepted the red tilak of kingship on his forehead. Finally, the queen, his mother, pinned a diamond brooch with a white feather on his turban, and he was ready to be seated on the throne.

The durbar hall was full. The courtiers could not take their eyes off the innocent face of their young king and the impressive figure of his mother seated next to him. Jindan smiled at Dalip. His boyish grin made her heart swell with pride. She prayed, 'Waheguru! Help us both to do justice to this seat of royalty.'

After the formalities of greetings and gifting were done, the whole of Lahore began celebrating. People came from far and near to participate in the festivities. There was revelry all around.

The people adored their little king. The Khalsa army roared in one voice, 'Waheguru, bless our maharaja! Jai Rani Jindan!'

The responsibility of managing the kingdom rested wholly with Rani Jindan. Dalip was but a child.

'Let him enjoy the glamour of being a king for now. I'll look after the affairs of the kingdom on his behalf,' she told herself.

The council of ministers pledged their support for her. But how much could she count on them? Would they wholeheartedly accept her as their reigning queen until Dalip came of age? With such doubts in her mind, she began her duties as regent.

It did not take Jindan long to realize that she needed to artfully steer in and out of complicated political situations at every turn.

Rani Jindan Kaur presented herself in the durbar every morning. She was always dressed in white to remind herself and the chieftains of their late maharaja Ranjit Singh. She wanted them to remember that they still owed their allegiance to the maharaja in preserving the power of Punjab.

Dalip too would go along with his mother to the durbar and keenly observe the proceedings. But Jindan would soon send him back to the palace for his lessons. She was strict about his education. He studied various subjects, including politics and warfare, with the best of teachers. Jindan herself remained in court for a good part of the day to discuss various state issues with the ministers.

Not long after, Jindan found that trouble had started brewing in the kingdom, and matters were coming to a head now.

'Walls have ears, Maharani-ji,' the chief minister, who was also called the wazir, warned her.

She knew it only too well. Ranjit Singh had often told her about the spies who were caught by him and dealt with severely. These spies were dangerous men who passed on information about internal problems to outsiders, especially the British, who were only too ready to use such knowledge to their advantage and attack.

Jindan and the ministers scrutinized the layout of the territory on a detailed map to ascertain where the British army was stationed. Then, they spent hours planning strategies to attack and make the enemy pull back. More often than not, the strategies worked, and the enemy was kept at bay. The ministers were pleased with their queen's shrewdness. They admired her mental fortitude and strength of purpose. Even the British were astonished at the queen-regent's astuteness.

At times, Jindan felt sorry for missing out on Dalip's bedtime stories, but it was more important for her to safeguard the kingdom that had been gifted to her son.

Rani Jindan's growing popularity infuriated some groups within the kingdom. Dalip's half-brother desperately wanted to replace him. The wazir was becoming increasingly high-handed. Jindan came to know through her informers that the wazir and a few other influential opponents were conspiring with the British to overthrow her.

It was becoming difficult for Jindan to maintain her position as the regent. Undaunted, she took some bold steps to set things right. First, she replaced the wazir, appointing her own brother in his place. Then, she put her faithful maid in charge of Dalip and told her to keep a watchful eye on him. She suspected there was danger lurking at every corner for her and her son. The kingdom that her husband had valorously established had to be protected at any cost. She told herself that not a shade of fear should seep into Dalip's mind. It would ruin his future. She prayed sincerely for courage and inspiration to perform her tasks.

Fortunately, the Khalsa army stayed true to her. They were ready to face any attack on the kingdom for her sake and for the sake of Punjab. Their shouts of 'Long live Rani Jindan! Long live Maharaja Dalip!' boosted her spirits. The Khalsa army's battles were truly fierce, so much so that the British Army absolutely dreaded them.

Not very long afterwards, Rani Jindan found that the number of people who were against her in the kingdom was growing steadily. The ministers who she thought were faithful suddenly turned against her and joined hands with the British. They killed her brother too.

It was easy for the British to attack Lahore now. They reached the outskirts of the city loaded with arms and ammunitions. The Khalsa army lost many soldiers in the fight. Exhausted in mind and body, those who had managed to escape enemy guns went to report matters to an alarmed Jindan. Young Dalip stood next to her clasping her hand. Trying her best to remain calm, she reminded him of his brave father.

'You have to be as strong as your father. He was known as the Lion of Punjab. You, the lion cub, should grow up to be an equally strong lion.' She kissed him lightly on his forehead, and then they went out to meet the soldiers.

Rani Jindan was distressed to see the soldiers' condition. Dalip looked up at his mother in confusion. There were a few long moments of terrifying silence.

Then, Jindan cried out, 'You are the guardians of our proud kingdom, which the maharaja loved more than himself and protected with all his heart and strength. Remember him, and go forth to do what each of us must to save our land from the greedy and untrustworthy British. See, the prince looks up to you to safeguard his future.' The queen's strong voice resonated all around. With bated breath, she waited for the soldiers to respond.

Time ticked slowly. Suddenly, a voice cried, 'We will continue to fight for the glory of Punjab, Maharani-ji. *Jo bole so nihal*! *Sat sri akal*!' Others joined him and their war cry rent the air.

Jindan breathed in relief. Perhaps Dalip's terrified look helped to motivate the men and revive their strength to fight. She thanked them, fed them well and saw them off to the battlefield with a heartfelt prayer on her lips.

Within a short time, the war became a painfully one-sided one. The British marched into Lahore. They confronted the queen. There was a war of words, but Jindan refused to make any political compromises.

Ultimately, it was of no use. The British made Dalip sign a treaty, which stated that the charge of Punjab now rested with them.

One last time, Rani Jindan Kaur sat on the throne with King Dalip on her lap. The durbar hall looked desolate. Just a handful of faithful courtiers gave them company. There was nothing left to do.

What next? Jindan thought. She drove away bleak thoughts of the future. They would only make her heart heavier. She wondered what Dalip was thinking. Surely, he would know that everything had changed. The astrologer's prediction pricked her heart like a poisoned arrow. *The time of the prince's birth is inauspicious… He will lose all…* She had never ever believed in astrological predictions… Until now.

Jindan took Dalip to Ranjit Singh's samadhi. She knelt before the tomb and wrapped her arm around her son. The young prince stood next to her with a bewildered expression.

With tearful eyes Jindan said softly, 'I'm sorry, sarkar. You know I tried my best to hold on to the powerful kingdom that you built and nurtured. I remembered and practised all that you taught me about governance and looked after our precious land for three years. But…I could not stand up against the betrayal of some of our own and the unscrupulous ways of the British. Your Khalsa were brave and patriotic to the very end.' Jindan's voice was choked while Dalip sobbed silently. Pale-faced, she turned to him. For a moment, both smiled through their tears. One last time, Jindan whispered to herself, 'I'm sorry, sarkar.'

Dalip hugged his mother tightly. The warmth of her child's love and a sudden whiff of cool breeze carrying the scent of forgiveness made the colour rush back to Jindan's face.